"*Parenting Without Pressure* is a very caring, insightful, and pragmatic way to view parenting. It provides concrete tools that take the power struggles out of parent-child interactions and allows more emphasis on positive exchanges of love and enjoyment of each other. As a parent, I no longer fear the adolescent time coming in my son's life."

—PENNY NORKUS, PARENT

"*Parenting Without Pressure* has the key ingredients for success: it requires interaction between the child and the parent and asks all involved to delay acting on their negative feelings as a means of seeing just how unimportant and insignificant our negative feelings can be. Further, it sets the stage for true praise and encouragement to be spread around generously."

—RANDY LEWIS, M.A., CHILDREN'S SERVICES COUNSELOR

"Parents often wait until their child is in high school to try to enforce rules of the household. By then, it's often too late to start to regain control. *Parenting Without Pressure* has helped some of my students' parents establish fair, enforceable rules."

—LISA BLISS, GUIDANCE COUNSELOR

"This innovative approach to consistency in parenting can be useful in parenting all types of children, not just the 'difficult' child. My experience tells me that consistency is the earmark of good parenting and this program is a miracle in assisting parents in providing that consistency."

—FREDERIC SEBERT, SUPERVISOR, HRS-UNIT 307

"*Parenting Without Pressure* has been a life saver for teaching parents easy and effective methods of discipline. It also drives home important messages about love, communication, and fairness."

—LINDA SILVERSTEIN, I.C.C.P., GREAT OAKS VILLAGE

"*Parenting Without Pressure* has been my light at the end of the tunnel. Teresa gives real tools to help us get closer to our kids and make them accountable."

—SUSAN H. ROSE, PARENT

"*Parenting Without Pressure* provides a practical, easy-to-understand and effective guide for both parents and their children. It allows for parenting to take place without the pitfalls that often occur when emotionally charged interactions take place. I have seen families become functional and united using this tool even after other efforts failed."

—TED SAUNDERS, ASSISTANT DEPARTMENT MANAGER, GREAT OAKS VILLAGE

"As a parent of three and a psychologist in a large public school system, I have used *Parenting Without Pressure* both professionally and personally. This workbook is the most useful, easy to understand, and easy to implement material I have had the opportunity to use and recommend."

—SHARON McGUIRE, PARENT AND SCHOOL PSYCHOLOGIST

"This book and Teresa's workshops are practical, interesting, and adaptable for most any parenting situation. I highly recommend this book for parents, teachers, and professionals."

—JOSEPH TRIM, M.A., LICENSED MENTAL HEALTH COUNSELOR

"*Parenting Without Pressure* is a unique, innovative parenting tool. When used with consistency and commitment, it will improve communication and cooperation even in the severest of conduct and oppositional-defiant disorders. *Parenting Without Pressure* is based on mutually agreed upon problems and goals, and therefore works to increase a child or adolescent's self-esteem in a 'win-win' situation."

—MARJORIE WILDE, COORDINATOR OF CHILDREN'S RESOURCE CENTER

"As a therapist in a children's crisis stabilization unit, I work daily with parents whose children are out of control. *Parenting Without Pressure* has given me specific techniques I can share with my clients. As a parent, I find that my 13-year-old daughter is evidence that these techniques really work."

—MELANIE STEIN, M.A., MENTAL HEALTH COUNSELOR

"In this uncertain world, it is reassuring to know that some of the people do have answers to some of the questions! Parents can now turn to *Parenting Without Pressure* for guidance in the most difficult job of raising children amid today's uncertainties. I heartily recommend the program to family and friends as well as to clients."

—SHELBY F. MORRISON, PH.D., PUBLIC SCHOOL PROGRAM SPECIALIST

"Through Mrs. Langston's experiences, examples, and guidance, we have been able to spend more time listening, loving, and enjoying our children. We recommend this book highly."

—KEVIN AND EVELYN WARREN, PARENTS

"As a school guidance counselor and psychotherapist who has worked exclusively with 'at risk' students and their families for 16 years, I can state unequivocally that the *Parenting Without Pressure* materials have consistently and effectively made the difference."

—J. LEE RIGLEY, SCHOOL GUIDANCE COUNSELOR AND PSYCHOTHERAPIST

"I can't say enough good things about the Parenting Without Pressure program. It has helped to restore structure and communication in our family and has reduced the stress level tremendously. We are extremely grateful to Teresa Langston and this program that she has provided to the public."

—LOUISE NELSON, PARENT

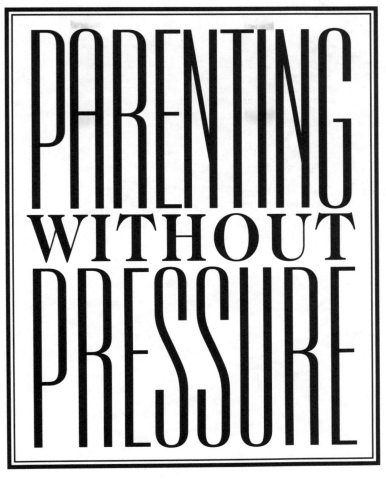

PARENTING WITHOUT PRESSURE

A WHOLE FAMILY APPROACH

TERESA A. LANGSTON

PIÑON PRESS

P.O. Box 35007, Colorado Springs, Colorado 80935

Library of Congress Catalog Card Number:
    94-65638
ISBN 08910-97503

Interior illustrations: Paige Braddock

Some of the anecdotal illustrations in this book
are true to life and are included with the permission of the persons involved. All other illustrations are composites of real situations, and
any resemblance to people living or dead is coin-
cidental.

Printed in the United States of America

    6 7 8 9 10 11 12 13 14 15 / 99 98

Contents

PART TWO: THE FAMILY WORKBOOK

To my wonderful daughter Heather,
who chose to use her will of iron and tenacious personality
to make a positive difference in the world

Acknowledgments

Writing *Parenting Without Pressure* has truly been a labor of love. However, I would never have been able to accomplish it without the assistance of some pretty wonderful folks.

I would like to extend a special thanks to Dr. William Brown, who encouraged me to put the Parenting Without Pressure concept in manuscript form. Bill has been a continual source of inspiration, and if it weren't for him, this book would not exist.

A special thanks to Trish Harris, who is responsible for introducing me to the great folks at Piñon Press. In addition to sharing with me her talents for marketing and business development, Trish has been a wonderful friend.

Also, I would like to thank my family, especially my daughter Renee, who provided me with much insight during the ten years we implemented the PWOP program with her.

Finally, I would like to extend my love and gratitude to my mentor, best friend, and husband, Herb. I will forever be grateful for his ability to put a positive spin on the most difficult of situations, and for teaching me the true meaning of unconditional love.

Foreword

It was with delight that I reviewed Teresa Langston's *Parenting Without Pressure*. The vision, knowledge, and innovations that she provides in this how-to book are outstanding. As one of Mrs. Langston's former professors, I am justifiably proud of the tool she has created for parents to restore and maintain positive family relationships.

In this rapidly changing world, it is so easy for young people to edge into serious problems. Often they become caught in a tangle of problems that seem insurmountable to them and their parents. What is so wonderful about *Parenting Without Pressure* is that sensible, practical strategies to reestablish order and tranquility in the home are spelled out clearly. Desperate parents immediately see a glimmer of hope, a way out of the despair they have long experienced.

Teresa Langston's workbook has provided many parents with sound guidance and needed structure for restoring seriously eroded relationships, enabling parents and offspring once again to enjoy family life. However, I believe *Parenting Without Pressure* makes an even more valuable contribution to families by avoiding serious problems before they begin.

As you study and apply the strategies and principles presented here, you will almost immediately sense a renewal of love and respect among family members that might have been eroded by the everyday hassles that get in the way of caring relationships.

William R. Brown, Ph.D.
Professor of Sociology

*"By wisdom a house is built
and by understanding
it is established;
and by knowledge
the rooms are filled
with all precious and pleasant riches."*

Proverbs 24:3-4
New American Standard Bible

PART ONE

Help for Pressured Kids

Guiding them around today's temptations.

Today's world is very different from the world children knew a generation ago. It's a difficult time to be a young person. Youngsters today are on the front line of a fast-changing world where clear definitions of right and wrong are no longer in place. Words such as *crack* and *AIDS* and *gang-banging* have been added to

vocabularies as kids are forced to make decisions unknown to the same age group a generation ago: Do I want to drink or take drugs? Have sex? Join a gang? Bring a gun to school? Should I stay in school? Unfortunately, it is easy for even the best of kids to find themselves overwhelmed as they struggle to make good choices.

Current research reveals how difficult that struggle can be.

- The Fullerton, California, police department and the state's department of education reported that the top offenses in school were drug abuse, alcohol abuse, pregnancy, suicide, rape, robbery, and assault.[1]
- Of 2,508 students polled in ninety-six schools across the United States, fifteen percent said they carried a handgun in the past thirty days.[2]
- During the past twenty years, the homicide rate doubled among ten-to-fourteen-year-old children. Homicide is the leading cause of death among African-American teens between ages fifteen and nineteen.[3]
- In the same time span,

suicide rates tripled among ten-to-fourteen-year-olds and doubled among fifteen-to-nineteen-year-olds.[4]

- Sixty-five percent of boys and fifty-one percent of girls are sexually active by the time they reach eighteen. About fifty percent do not use contraceptives the first time they have intercourse.[5]
- For women nineteen years old and younger, births outside of marriage have increased from fifteen to fifty-one percent over the last two decades.[6]
- About 4½ million teenagers between fourteen and seventeen years old are problem drinkers. One out of every three high school seniors gets drunk on weekends. And drunk-driving accidents are the number-one killer of young people ages fifteen to twenty-four.[7]

Yes, it's a difficult time for kids. But it's also a difficult time for parents. It's tough guiding children around these obstacles. Families often find themselves adrift, without focus or direction because yesterday's parenting techniques no longer work. It's hard to find effective solutions and we worry about discovering them too late.

If you're struggling with a difficult child, there's hope for you. *Parenting Without Pressure* can help you establish a structure that restores normal family living and prepares kids to meet today's challenges. This book offers practical parenting techniques that focus on discipline, communication, self-

esteem, and unconditional love. In turn, these techniques teach children accountability, responsibility, and consequences for behavior.

THINGS PARENTING WITHOUT PRESSURE WILL HELP YOU DO

- Establish rules and boundaries for each of your children.
- Arbitrate parent/child differences and create workable solutions.
- Teach children how to solve problems and make good choices.
- Make kids accountable for their time away from home.
- Communicate daily about chores and expectations.
- Discuss "anything and everything" important to you and your kids.

However, this book isn't just for parents with challenging children. *Parenting Without Pressure* can work for anyone who wants to practice pro-active parenting skills. In particular, the family workbook presents a way to be firm, fair, and consistent with discipline. It has also helped parents eliminate family fighting, enhance their children's self-esteem, and create a more positive home life.

Developed as my family struggled with an out-of-control child, *Parenting Without Pressure* provided us with a win/win format to modify our daughter's negative behavior. It also enabled us to shift our focus, thus allowing us to reinforce the good behavior we wanted Heather to repeat, express our unconditional love for her, and underscore her immeasurable worth as a person. With these principles we were finally able to recapture the positive aspects of our family life.

And that is the reward of *Parent-ing Without Pressure*. It takes the hassle out of parenting so your home can be the haven it's meant to be.

CHAPTER ONE

Home Sweet Battleground

Bringing structure to a faltering family.

I'd always thought of us as a typical family. If we weren't like Ozzie and Harriet, we were at least like the Brady Bunch.

When I married my husband, Herb, we blended nicely into a

middle-class family. As a widow I brought eighteen-month-old Heather to our marriage and Herb, a divorced father, added his three children on the weekends. Later a beautiful baby daughter joined us and we all adored her. As our children grew over the years, we experienced ups and downs and everyday hassles, but nothing we thought was extreme. Because Herb and I were happy and content, we thought our kids felt that way, too.

Unfortunately, fourteen-year-old Heather did not. She was miserable, and I'm embarrassed to admit we missed it. Heather created her share of crises, but we chalked them up to adolescence. Ironically, for a while I'd been receiving "problem" phone calls from school about Heather. If someone called and asked me if I was Mrs. Langston, I wanted to ask, "Who wants to know?" If the call concerned Heather, I didn't want to be Mrs. Langston!

But we weren't seriously alarmed and referred to these incidents as our strong-willed daughter's "problem of the day." For too long, we assumed Heather's daily problems constituted a passing phase or peer pressure, but certainly nothing serious.

Looking back, I realize that warning signs clearly indicated our

Heather was in trouble. She stayed in a constant state of rebellion and refused to have anything to do with the family. She acquired a new set of friends and drastically changed her appearance. She also had problems with her teachers at school and her grades took a nose dive. But unfortunately, we refused to see the red flags and her problems grew worse.

It wasn't until one of Heather's high school teachers confronted us that we recognized our daughter's behavior was serious and troubled. The teacher told us Heather was failing the ninth grade, sexually acting out, and experimenting with alcohol and drugs. Finally, somebody had yanked us out of denial and into the frightening truth. It was as if we'd allowed Heather to dive into a pool without teaching her how to swim. Worse yet, we'd stood by passively and watched her almost drown.

Heather's behavior continued to deteriorate and she rapidly spiraled out of control. With each act of rebellion, I reacted by becoming more authoritarian in my discipline. As I tightly held the reins and struggled for control, Heather grew more angry and defiant.

The emotional atmosphere in our family disintegrated rapidly, and soon our home resembled a battleground rather than the safe, secure, and nurturing place where our children could grow and mature. Almost everything that was being said and done was ugly, negative, and destructive. There were daily screaming matches, slammed doors, and hurt feelings—and anger and resentment grew like an ugly disease. Everyday I promised myself that "today" was going to be different. I even practiced things to say to Heather when she got home from school so we wouldn't fight. But as always, something triggered the horrifying pattern and we hopelessly argued.

Everybody was miserable. And Heather, with her belligerent spirit, "I-don't-give-a-damn" attitude, and four-letter-word vocabulary, was the most miserable of all. Years later she shared how difficult those days really were for her. She said, "Mom, every time I got off the school bus, I would feel sick to my stomach and wanted to throw up." I knew exactly how she felt, because when she came home, I wanted to throw up too. What a horrible mess we were in!

DESPERATELY SEEKING STRUCTURE

If we couldn't help Heather or ourselves, we thought maybe someone else could. Fortunately, we had enough wits left to find an excellent therapist. Individually and as a family, we were in counseling for about a year. During this time, Herb and I learned many new parenting concepts and techniques.

But long after Herb and I understood the principles of good parenting, we were still left with the dilemma of *how* to put them into practice! For example, we desperately needed to shore up the structure in our home and to be consistent in disciplining our children. We needed to pull our family together, provide Heather with safe boundaries, and establish open lines of communication. Still looking for answers, we read countless articles, journals, and books—and tried what felt like almost everything. But for months we still practiced hit-and-miss parenting, with more "miss" than "hit."

The turning point came when Herb and I realized we'd never developed a plan of action or strategy for raising our children. Nor had we ever defined our goals and objectives in terms of our family. . . . Oh, we often had talked about our hopes and dreams for our individual children. But we had never discussed seriously how we could help them develop into mature, responsible adults.

Both my husband and I are professional people. After dinner we sometimes talk for hours about our projects, carefully outlining our plans of action. We spend time in planning because we know success doesn't just happen. It results from careful forethought and deliberate action. However, never once did we take that kind of logic and apply it to our family—until the circumstances became desperate. For the first time, we took a hard look at the reality of our family situation and began to establish realistic, workable goals, not only for our children but also for ourselves.

As parents, we decided our overall goal was simply to "deparent" our children; that is, move them from being self-centered, dependent (and/or out-of-control) young people to being self-reliant, independent adults. And to accomplish this, we needed to teach them everything necessary to function well as adults: things such as the important correlation between their behavior and its consequences (both good and bad), the concepts of accountability and responsibility, and appro-

priate ways to solve problems and make good choices.

BASIC PARENTING PRINCIPLES

Upon reviewing these goals, Herb and I realized that many of our parenting principles were based on common sense concepts that we had learned by simple observation. We literally had grown up with them as they had been passed from one generation to the next. Others, however, were based on things learned more

BASIC PARENTING PRINCIPLES

1. Children of all ages thrive with structure and boundaries. They need to know the rules and consequences of breaking those rules.
2. They also need the security of consistent, fair discipline.
3. Parents should always strive to separate children from their behavior. In other words, kids should clearly understand that although their behavior might be inappropriate or undesirable, they never are!
4. Healthy families are built through good communication which is more than hearing and understanding. Good communication involves creating a safe atmosphere that allows family members to express their thoughts and feelings.
5. Kids need positive affirmation and unconditional love to build their self-esteem.
6. Children learn more by what their parents do than by what they say. Therefore, parents should always strive to be great role models for good behavior.

recently as we searched for methods of coping with Heather's challenging behavior.

Herb and I also discussed character traits or values we would like our children to acquire along the way. We based our list of character traits on the advice of Beth Winship, syndicated columnist for the *Los Angeles Times*, who writes a column called "Growing Pains."

CREATING THE WORKBOOK

Once Herb and I had determined exactly what we wanted to teach Heather, we developed a systematic way to accomplish it. As Heather's parents, we set about the task of writing what has become the *Parenting Without Pressure* workbook.

This workbook enabled us to parent with consistency, tackle behavioral problems appropriately, and develop meaningful character traits in our children. In addition, it provided us with a tangible, constructive tool that was objective, fair, and non-manipulative. And because the workbook enabled us to write down those things Heather perceived as negative (such as rules and consequences), what we said to her could be positive and uplifting. It literally allowed us to parent without pressure.

Putting together the first workbook was truly a labor of love for Heather. Piece by piece, we added sections to the workbook as we worked on her behavior. And when we saw the first positive changes in Heather, we began using the workbook as a preventive measure with our younger daughter.

As the months passed and Heather's behavior continued to improve, I received phone calls from parents desperate for help with their children. First, the parents of Heather's friends called and then strangers asked for help. They, too, found that the workbook's structure helped them consistently modify their kids' inappropriate behavior and reinforced desirable actions. Gradually their homes were turning into positive places to live.

As word of the workbook's success spread through Central Florida, local churches and schools sponsored workshops and seminars. Today, throughout the United States, psychiatric hospitals, juvenile courts, and other agencies and organizations use the workbook with families. And families as far away as Australia and Malta utilize the workbook strategy.

But first let me say if you're a frustrated parent, don't give up. People who attend my Parenting Without Pressure seminars often ask, "How is Heather doing today?" She is doing extremely well, and we are very proud of her. Heather is a graduate student pursuing a degree in family and marriage counseling and working with troubled adolescents. Oh, Heather is still very strong-willed, but now that strong will is tempered with patience and maturity. Best of all, Heather is more than a daughter to me; she's become a wonderful friend.

Herb and I can't take credit for Heather's success; she made it possible. Herb and I merely implemented simple steps that created safe parameters for Heather as she walked through some very difficult times. These steps helped us build a bridge across the chasm of a very troubled adolescence and make it to the other side as friends.

HOMEWORK FOR PARENTS

Before proceeding to chapter 2, take time to consider a strategy for raising your children.

1. Define your parenting goals. What is the purpose of your parenting?

2. Review the list of basic parenting principles on page 21. How can these help you accomplish your parenting goals?

3. Examine "Traits Teens Should Learn on Their Way to Maturity" (below). How can you promote the development of these traits with your children?

4. List ways you model good and bad behavior to your children.

TRAITS TEENS SHOULD LEARN ON THEIR WAY TO MATURITY

1. Responsibility. Realizing your actions always have consequences and making yourself accountable for what they are.
2. Self-control. Stopping to think what is a useful and suitable reaction in a given situation instead of just "popping off."
3. Looking ahead. Planning your life, not just around today's pleasures, but in terms of next week, next month, next year.
4. Understanding. Learning what others think and feel, and having concern for their welfare.
5. Motivation. Developing goals in your life, as well as the desire to work hard for them.
6. Decision making. Learning to judge a situation and make an intelligent and appropriate choice by evaluating the pluses and minuses, including your own values.
7. Love. Learning to give as well as receive love, and to share closeness and true concern, tenderness and loyalty.
8. Self-reliance. When you have developed the other traits, you will have enough faith in your own judgment and ability to run your life well, without dependence on your parents or other adults.
9. Confidence in oneself as an individual. Mature people value their own selves well enough to believe strongly in their values and goals. They care what other people think, but not to the point where they can be pressured into behavior they don't truly approve of for themselves.[1]

CHAPTER TWO

Your Kids and the Real World

Teaching responsibility with a family workbook.

We all live by rules. If you do not believe it, drive down the interstate at eighty-five mph, do not pay your taxes, or leave the dog in the house past potty time. Chances are very good that you are going to pay the consequences for all the above.

Children need to learn this concept early. Unfortunately for many, they do not learn this cause-and-effect concept until later in life—and often the hard way.

In a Central Florida study about juvenile delinquency and its correlation to substance abuse, it was found that many youths were surprised by their incarceration in a detention facility. Even though their individual rates of recidivism (repeated offenses) were high (an average of three times per juvenile), they attributed their return to a detention facility to a variety of external factors. Rarely did they attribute it to anything they had done.[1]

But overlooking personal responsibilities isn't a problem just for delinquent youngsters. As they grow toward maturity, all children need guidance in taking responsibility for their lives. And it's a parent's job to equip kids with the skills they need to move successfully from dependent children to independent adults. To do that, children should be given the privilege of doing things for themselves as early as possible. By taking increasing responsibility for picking up their toys, doing their laundry, managing their money, and getting to school on time, kids develop the necessary skills and self-confidence to manage their real world.

The *Parenting Without Pressure* workbook is divided into five sections designed to teach your children this increasing responsibility and to link their behavior to choices and consequences. As you review the workbook contents outlined in this chapter, keep in mind that you'll need to develop one workbook for each child in your home. This will allow you to target each child's needs and accommodate the differences among siblings.

SECTION 1: RULES WE CAN LIVE BY

Parents often expect children to internalize the norms or rules of the household without going to the trouble of writing things down. But this chancy internalization process often does not take place. When a child breaks a rule, parents often hear, "I didn't understand," or "I misunderstood," or "I forgot!" Heather was an equal match for the most clear-headed adult, so I was often convinced that I was either suffering memory loss or losing my mind. Because I feared both possibilities, I devised the first section of the workbook.

This section stresses two important concepts: arbitration and rules to live by. The rules and consequences for breaking them must be fair and relevant to the individual child. What needs to be written for one child can be left unsaid for another.

When you begin a *Parenting Without Pressure* workbook, start with no written rules. They are to be added only as a child gives evidence that they are needed. But once they are written down and the consequences are established, they are the bottom line.

Arbitration is a once-a-week time

that families set aside to objectively, openly, and fairly discuss anything in the children's workbooks. You can conduct family arbitrations that everyone attends and/or one-on-one meetings with each child. Individual arbitrations are helpful when older children have simultaneous activities outside the home or if sensitive and private issues need to be discussed. Whatever the circumstances, be sure that you have a regular, established arbitration time for each child in the family.

During arbitration, everything in a child's workbook is subject to discussion and/or change, and it's the only time during the week such discussions or changes are made. If you're consistent about this, almost all of the everyday hassles with your children will be eliminated. Arbitration is a time to create new rules if

RULES WE CAN LIVE BY

1. Rule: _Unplug your hot rollers after you use them._

   Consequence: _You will lose the use of them for one week._

2. Rule: _____

   Consequence: _____

3. Rule: _____

   Consequence: _____

necessary, acknowledge good behavior, and add new privileges. The following example shows the benefits of arbitration.

After using her hot rollers in the morning, Heather continually left them plugged in for long periods of time, if not all day. Because I feared a total meltdown in her bathroom, her forgetfulness turned into an everyday hassle. When I began to apply this concept from the workbook, the problem was eliminated. At arbitration I carefully explained to her why I wanted the rollers unplugged: They might burn down our house. We then established a rule that the hot rollers must be unplugged after every use. And together, we decided on a consequence: If Heather left them plugged in, she would lose the hot rollers for a week.

It wasn't two days until—you guessed it—Heather left her hot rollers plugged in. The matter was handled simply by writing a message in the "Daily Stuff" section of her workbook.

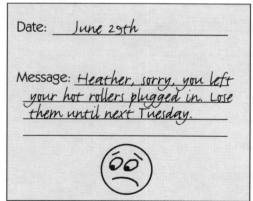

Date: _June 29th_

Message: _Heather, sorry, you left your hot rollers plugged in. Lose them until next Tuesday._

There wasn't much Heather could say. We had discussed the need for a rule, and we had mutually decided on a consequence. She left her hot rollers plugged in, and the consequence was the result of her behavior.

Unfortunately, parents can fall into two traps at this point.

1. They can allow themselves to get "hooked" in to discussing the consequence at the time the rule is broken. This will usually result in an argument.

2. They can take the path of least resistance and not follow through with the consequence. And they'll teach their children that rules and responsibilities don't matter.

So remember, to make the Parenting Without Pressure program work, you must be consistent every time! This might seem difficult at first. But once the kids get the idea that rules and consequences have been fairly and objectively established, and they stand until the next arbitration, those "everyday" hassles will cease. Everyone will know, up front, what is expected of them— every time—with no room for any misunderstandings!

One final note about arbitration. Upon starting the program, some children might be very angry and defensive at arbitration. However, hang in there! Once kids learn that the workbook and arbitration are there to stay, they will settle down and learn how to make it work for them.

When my husband and I first started having arbitrations with Heather, not only was her attitude defensive, but her four-letter-word vocabulary was put to extensive use. She soon learned, however, that arbitration occurred only weekly and it was fair, reasonable, and impartial. As she became an active participant, she quickly found that arbitration could be very beneficial for her.

By the time Heather left for college, she was articulate, well organized, and polite as she opted for her rule revisions or discussed whatever happened to be on her mind. In fact, I realized recently, she could have given any second-year law student a run for his money!

SECTION 2: FRIENDS AND FAMILY

It's horrible to discover at one o'clock in the morning that Mary, your daughter's best friend, has a different last name than her parents. Or Paul, your daughter's second best friend, has an unlisted phone number. You don't know where your daughter is . . . and you don't have the right phone numbers.

You can eliminate this dilemma by asking your kids to complete the second section of the workbook, "Friends and Family." In this section, they fill in the names and phone numbers of friends and their parents. Is Mary's last name different than her folks? No problem. Her

---

FRIENDS AND FAMILY

EMERGENCY NUMBERS
Police: 911   Fire: 911   Rescue Unit: 911
Family Doctor: _Dr. Clark 593-1301_

PARENTS AND RELATIVES
Mom at work: _530-3523_
Dad at work: _598-1214_
Relative: _Grandmother Stine 480-3551_
Relative: _Uncle Ron 955-7767_

PARENTS' FRIENDS
Name and number: _Mr. & Mrs. Baxter 598-7128_
Name and number: _Carol Bennett 366-7788_
Name and number: _____

NEIGHBORS
Name and number: _Mark Leming 594-2281_
Name and number: _Eva Kline 548-8630_
Name and number: _____

MY FRIENDS AND THEIR PARENTS
Friend's name and number: _Kirsten Williams 471-7817_
Friend's parent and number: _Helen Williams 471-7817_
Friend's name and number: _Joel Davis 599-7891_
Friend's parent and number: _Don Davis 599-7891_
Friend's name and number: _____
Friend's parent and number: _____

phone number is in the workbook. If Paul's phone number is unlisted, that's no problem, either. It's in the workbook too.

But this section isn't just for kids to list phone numbers. There's also space to list important phone numbers such as those for work, emergency services, and adult friends and family to call in a pinch. These are especially helpful for younger kids.

Finally, this section allows parents to network with one another. This is important because it allows you to exchange information, such as the specific details for a teenager's party. It also communicates your interest and concern as a parent!

SECTION 3: FUN TIMES AND EVENINGS OUT

After too many evenings of "But Mom, I know I told you that's where we were going," I devised the third section of the workbook. It's called "Fun Times and Evenings Out."

By utilizing this section when older children leave the house to join their friends, you will know exactly where they will be, who they will be

with, and what time to expect them home. That's because the kids write this information in the workbook before they leave. This leaves no room for misunderstandings. The facts are in the workbook.

Signing out provides safeguards for the kids, too. One evening Heather and her friends ended up

---

FUN TIMES AND EVENINGS OUT

Date: _9-12-86_

Time leaving/returning: _7:00-12:00 p.m._

Where I will be: _Football game &_
Burger King

Friends I will be with: _Mary & Paul_

Date: _____

Time leaving/returning: _____

Where I will be: _____

Friends I will be with: _____

Date: _____

Time leaving/returning: _____

Where I will be: _____

Friends I will be with: _____

spending several hours in jail. When I arrived at the police station, Heather was a pathetic sight. She was frantic and her eyes were swollen from crying. The first thing she hysterically told me was, "It's in the workbook!!"

Heather was right. She'd been in the place and with the friends she listed in the workbook. Unfortunately, neither Heather nor I realized there was a nine o'clock curfew for that area. The trespassing charge stuck.

Someone once said that trust is something you earn and should never freely be given away. This workbook section also gives children the opportunity to earn trust based on their accountability and responsibility.

As a young teenager, Heather loved to skate, so often on Saturday I would drive her and her friends to the local skating rink. Although we always had a prearranged pick-up time, sometimes I would arrive early. Each time I checked and Heather was doing everything as promised, our trust relationship grew. When this happened, Heather loved it. She'd bring this incident to our next arbitration and gain additional privileges.

However, if I checked on Heather and the situation was not as promised, Herb and I would simply tighten the reigns and pull in her operating boundaries.

SECTION 4: DAILY STUFF

More than ten million American women are the head of their household.[2] Of married women with school-age children, more than 65 percent work outside the home.[3] Yet mom is still the primary caretaker of both the children and the household. And she needs help!

Early in life children can learn that everyone in the family needs to pull together to run the household smoothly. Dishes don't wash themselves, beds don't get made magically, and towels don't exit the dryer already folded.

In their "Daily Stuff" sections, you simply list the chores your children are expected to complete each day. For example, when there were eleven wet towels on Heather's bedroom floor, there was no problem. I just opened the workbook to the "Daily Stuff" section and wrote, "Heather, please wash, dry, and fold all the dirty towels. Thank you."

DAILY STUFF

Date: 9-8-89

Daily Stuff: Please

1. Give the dog a bath

2. Empty the dishwasher

3. _____

4. _____

Messages:

Hope you had a great day at school!

I will be home @ 4:30.

Please give Mrs. Smith a call. She wants to know if you can babysit tonight.

I love you!

Mom

When you list chores for kids, be sensitive to their schedules. Children who attend school all day essentially complete eight hours of work. If they also hold part-time jobs or attend extracurricular activities, they'll be tired. Chores are important, but one or two simple tasks (emptying the dishwasher, sweeping the floor) are probably enough for one day. Save your spring cleaning for the weekend!

We had an established rule pertaining to "Daily Stuff": "Your daily stuff must be completed by 4:30 or you lose the use of your phone, stereo, and TV for the remainder of the day and evening." This elimi-

nated the ritual of pleading, begging, and threatening before chores were completed.

Additionally, daily stuff provides children with many opportunities to learn responsibility. Ken Hsu, a psychiatric social worker at Meriter Hospital in Madison, Wisconsin, explains: "There are two kinds of responsibility. There's task-area responsibility which includes the jobs you do such as cleaning your room and doing your homework. And there is responsibility for yourself—knowing what is right and wrong. Because children think more concretely than abstractly, it is easier for them to grasp the more concrete area of task responsibility. The more proficient they become in this area, the more capable they will become at the abstract job of being responsible for themselves."[4]

Also important, daily stuff gives children many opportunities to gain confidence. Many parents use daily planners at work to remind them of tasks to be completed. If you ask how they feel after working their way through a list of things to do, their response is always the same—"GREAT!" Completing daily stuff produces the same feeling for kids. They feel good and confident about what they have accomplished.

The added bonus from this "Daily Stuff" section is that it provides a perfect place for messages. Many children today arrive home hours before their parents do, and it's nice to come home to a friendly note that says "Hello. There's a treat for you in the refrigerator" or "I love you."

With this section, parents can reinforce what is positive and enhance a child's self-esteem. For example, a parent might want to comment on a particular job that was done well: "You did a wonderful job cleaning the bathroom yesterday. I especially liked the floor. Thanks!" One mom left this message: "I am a POSITIVE THINKER. Say it ten times and ask me for $5.00." The woman's son called her at the office immediately and said it ten times!

SECTION 5:
ANYTHING AND EVERYTHING GOES

Think of this last section as a miscellaneous drawer where you and your kids put all sorts of unrelated but not-to-be-forgotten things. Literally it's a place where "anything and everything goes." For instance, in this section of Heather's workbook we kept track of progress reports, family contracts, and those things we needed to discuss at arbitration.

Weekly Progress Reports

To monitor Heather's performance at school, we required that she bring home a progress report. During the two years that we tracked Heather's progress, we simply required her to earn a C, or 2.0 grade point average, for the week in each of her subjects. This earned her the privilege of going out with friends on weekends. Each Friday it was Heather's responsibility to take the progress report to each of her teachers. And because we requested weekly reports at parent/teacher conferences, Heather's teachers readily provided the information.

Heather's C average may not seem suitable for your children, but it was a realistic goal for her at that stage. This was the only way we got Heather out of the ninth grade.

If you have to make a similar decision for one of your children, your frame of reference should be: (1) where your child is starting

---

WEEKLY PROGRESS REPORT

Name: Ann

For week of: February 7-11

Class period	Subject	Teacher	Numerical grade point average
1st	Spanish	Wilson	2.8
2nd	Algebra	Webb	1.9
3rd	Science	Jamison	2.0
4th	Art	Miller	2.4
5th	English Lit.	Johnson	2.1
6th			

CONTRACT

Name: _Heather_

Subject: _Tickets for speeding_

Desired Behavior: _Be a responsible driver._

How it will be accomplished: _Pay to go to driving school. Also pay tickets by working at home._

Consequences: _You will lose your license_

Heather Langston   _5/21/86_

Child's Signature: Date:

Herb Langston   _5/21/86_

Parent's Signature: Date:

---

academically; (2) what he or she can realistically obtain.

Family Contracts

At one time, it seemed Heather was on a first-name basis with every police officer within twenty miles of our home. After she received several tickets, Herb and I decided enough was enough. We asked her to draw up a contract stating how she planned to be a more responsible driver and, of course, pay her tickets. We all agreed on the terms, signed the document, and placed it in the "Anything and Everything Goes" section of the workbook.

Don't hesitate to make similar contracts with your kids. They model and teach responsibility.

THINGS TO DISCUSS
AT ARBITRATION

Use this page to list things that should be discussed at arbitration. Whether they are troublesome areas that need correcting or behavior that should be praised, you can eliminate the possibility of forgetting them simply by listing them here.

For example, my younger daughter, Renee, had trouble remembering to turn off the lights in her bedroom. We decided at arbitration that for every light she left on, I'd deduct fifty cents from her allowance. In the "Everything and Anything Goes" section, I kept track of the lights left on and how much allowance I owed her—or what amount she owed me at the end of the week!

**THINGS TO DISCUSS
AT ARBITRATION**

1. Date: _3/13 sarcastic note_
2. Date: _3/16 dirty dishes_
3. Date: _3/17 phone bill_
4. Date: _3/20 doing well in school_
5. Date: _3/20 missing blouse_
6. Date: _3/21 not fighting with sister_
7. Date: _____
8. Date: _____

MORE THAN JUST PAPER

A recent study indicated that most parent/child arguments involve mundane things such as chores, curfew, clothing, and homework.[5] Far too often, parents get sidetracked with these minor issues, resulting in a daily communication pattern of nagging and fighting. Because the workbook and arbitration provide a constructive format for resolving conflict, parents are free to develop supportive family relationships and create positive lines of communication.

Recently, a family shared how well this worked for them. Both parents worked and didn't arrive home till 6:30 p.m. By implementing the workbook system, they literally rediscovered their family! Freed from the ongoing "When are you going to do your homework?" or "Why haven't you taken out the trash?" type of communication that had prevailed for years, they could spend time getting to know their children. Family dinners and evenings were spent laughing, talking, and sharing their lives.

Another family found that by not continually fighting over little things, the family members were less defensive and therefore more responsive to open discussion about relevant topics such as peer pressure and social issues.

CHILDREN AND CHOICES

Once your children catch on that their behavior determines their personal freedom, you can take the concept one step further. You can help them understand that their behavior results from the choices they make. And even if your children have

chosen bad behavior in the past, they can choose good behavior now. Instead of reacting, which takes no thought, they can begin responding to situations by thinking them through.

Stopping to think is one of the most powerful tools you can teach your kids. Heather learned quickly that by thinking before acting, she could make great choices. And as her success rate grew, so did her confidence and ability to decide responsibly.

DIGGING FOR GOLD

Transforming kids into responsible people takes time and hard work. However, while they are developing their ability to make good choices, you can shift your focus to what they're doing right and the actions you want repeated.

Think for a minute about an old-time prospector. He'll probably shovel a great deal of dirt before he

ever hits gold. Yet despite the huge mounds of shoveled dirt, his attention never wavers. His focus on the gold is constant. You see, he is never sidetracked by the dirt because he always remembers the incredible value of the gold.

Unfortunately, parents can shovel a lot of "dirt" when dealing with children's negative behavior. However, if you always remember the importance of the "gold," you will be able to maintain your focus there.

This is more easily accomplished with the *Parenting Without Pressure* workbook. It provides the everyday structure that you need to cope with inappropriate behavior while you look for your children's best. This enabled us to shift our focus and spend our time and energy on Heather's good behavior and remind her that she really was capable of accomplishing wonderful things.

MAKING YOUR *PWOP* WORKBOOKS

Children in families always come in an assortment of shapes, sizes, and ages, with a variety of temperaments and personalities. Parents will find that a rule that has to be written for one child can be left unsaid for another child. That is one reason workbook contents will vary from child to child. Because of this, it's necessary to make a workbook for each child, following these steps:

1. Purchase a five-tab spiral notebook, the kind often sold at grocery stores. One should last about four months.

2. On each of the tabbed pages, write the name of a workbook sec-tion: (a) Rules We Can Live By; (b) Friends and Family; (c) Fun Times and Evenings Out; (d) Daily Stuff; (e) Anything and Everything Goes.

3. An alternate method is to use a three-ring binder and copy the workbook pages found in Appendix A. Simply add workbook sheets as needed.

4. For younger children, eliminate the sections that don't apply, such as the Friends part of Friends and Family, and Fun Times and Evenings Out. You probably know all your children's friends because they are next-door neighbors, and younger children usually don't have fun times and evenings out without Mom and Dad.

5. Ask older kids to fill in the information about their friends in Friends and Family. After they've used the program for awhile, some families simply recopy these lists from the previous workbooks. Our children kept a list of their friends on our home computer. With each new workbook, they simply revised their list, printed it, and stapled it in the Friends section of their new workbook.

6. When you start a new workbook, recopy only the rule pertaining to daily stuff and the general disobeying rule (see pages 29-30). Because both are utilized often, it's best to keep these handy. However, all the other rules from past workbooks should stay in effect. Ideally, by now, they have been internalized and are permanently deposited where they should have been all along—in the children's memory banks!

SUGGESTIONS ABOUT
HOW TO USE
PARENTING WITHOUT PRESSURE

These guidelines will help the workbook system run smoothly for your family.

1. At the first family meeting, explain the program and the workbooks. Focus on the positive aspects and the benefits to everyone. Be sure to say this is a win/win strategy that tangibly emphasizes behavior and its consequences, both positive and negative. Set the time for your next meeting, allowing everyone the opportunity to prepare for it.

2. The second time your family meets, create individual *Parenting Without Pressure* workbooks with your children. As you create each section, explain it again so everyone understands how the section works. Give the children the opportunity to discuss their concerns and problem areas. Then discuss your specific areas of concern. Establish a specific time for upcoming arbitrations.

3. As the family familiarizes itself with the workbook during the first week of implementation, use only the Rules We Can Live By and the Daily Stuff sections. This will give everyone the opportunity to begin to understand the program and prepare for the first arbitration.
    Some parents find it necessary to start with rules concerning daily stuff and willful disobedience. When you present these for the first time, follow these examples:

Daily stuff rule: "Daily stuff must be completed by (specific time). If that does not happen, (specific consequence)." Without this rule, you could be asking, pleading, and begging your children to complete their assigned chores.

Disobeying rule: "Any willful act of disobedience will result in (consequence)." This rule covers inappropriate behavior that currently does not have a rule/consequence. (The disobeying clause is discussed more fully on page 45).

4. The second week will be the toughest. It's not unusual for some children, especially teenagers, to attempt to sabotage the program during week two. But hang in there! Once everyone realizes it's a permanent part of family life, the kids will settle down and make it work for them.

5. Arbitration Day is just that. Listen to the kids. Be as fair as you can. Try to address their needs every time. Let them help formulate their own rules and consequences. Remember, however, that you are the parent, and the final decision about anything rests with you.

6. Refuse any challenges to do battle outside of arbitration. Allow the rules, consequences, daily stuff, and contracts to take effect without comment during the week. And don't try to "outfight kids" at arbitration. You can't! But you can out think them. Simply ask yourself, "What do I want to see happen here, and how can I accomplish it?"

7. Be consistent and follow through every time. Children can be tough and manipulative. Once they learn to badger a parent out of consequences, a contract, or daily stuff, you have lost the ball game.

8. Keep workbooks in a central area such as the kitchen. When the kids carry them off to other parts of the house, they often get lost. The workbooks need to be in a location where they will be seen often by the children (perhaps the kitchen table) because they're responsible for reading the workbooks and accomplishing their daily stuff.

9. Each evening, fill out the Daily Stuff section for the next day. This eliminates additional stress in the morning when you are trying to get the family to work and school on time. Always write a note, even when you don't assign chores. Not only is it a great way to remind a child that you love him and enhance his self-esteem, but also it helps a child develop the habit of reading his notebook.

10. Remind your children often that there is no "split camp" in your home. You're all on the same team. Frequently remind them of your love. Continually look for the best in your kids and when you find it always show it to them.

HOMEWORK FOR PARENTS

Before the first family meeting, review the Parenting Without Pressure program and make notes so you can describe it and explain why your family will begin using it.

CHAPTER THREE

Rules We Can Live By

Establishing effective rules and boundaries.

Imagine you're driving a car on a two-lane bridge over a river. What side of the road do you drive on? Now imagine you're crossing the bridge again a few days later. The night before, a storm washed out the guard rails. What side will you drive on this time? You'll probably switch from staying on the right side to hug-

ging the middle of the road unless traffic comes from the opposite direction. Though you did not realize it, the guard rails had provided you with a sense of security.

Structure is like that for children. In a real and practical sense, providing structure is the most "freeing" thing you can do for kids. It offers safety and gives guidance so they can grow and mature. It helps them learn about consequences and behavior. And within secure parameters, it teaches them to exercise good judgment. You can build this emotionally secure structure for your children by establishing operating boundaries and household rules for them.

SETTING BOUNDARIES

Operating boundaries are the parameters in which children can safely and reasonably conduct their lives and grow toward maturity. These boundaries include responsibilities, which are those behaviors you require from your children, and privileges, which are the acknowledgments your children receive for responsible behavior. For example, older children are responsible for returning home by a certain time at night. If they consistently stay within

THE BASICS OF BOUNDARIES

School night curfews	■ Kids should be home by dinner, except for specific activities approved by parents.
Weekend and holiday curfews	■ Sixth grade: 10:00 p.m. ■ Seventh and eighth grades: 10:00 to 11:30 p.m. ■ Ninth and tenth grades: 11:00 p.m. to midnight. ■ Eleventh and twelfth grades: 11:00 p.m. to 12:30 a.m. ■ Curfews should not exceed 12:30 a.m. unless there's a special occasion. ■ Be awake or have your kids wake you up when they get home.
Dating ages	■ High school: dates should be no more than two years older than your child. ■ Middle school: supervised group activities only. ■ Double dating: age 15. ■ Single dating: age 16.
Other activities	■ Teenage nightclubs: teens 17 or 18 years old. ■ Peer parties: middle and high school students should never attend unchaperoned parties. Obtain the host parents' names, address, and phone number. Call ahead and verify the occasion and ask questions about supervision and the alcohol and drug policy. ■ Rock concerts: older teens can attend together if they're fulfilling their responsibilities. Younger teens never without adult supervision. ■ Mall shopping: all right for older teens. Younger teens only for a short period of unsupervised time.

this boundary, they could receive the privilege of staying out an hour later on the weekends.

Boundaries Based on Age

Generally, two factors will affect your children's boundaries. The first and most obvious is age because it's a measure of their maturity. Seven-year-olds can't possibly carry the same responsibilities as sixteen-year-olds, so their boundaries take different shapes.

For many parents, age-appropriate boundaries can be difficult to discern. In the box on this page is a list of boundaries suggested by Dr. John Crocitto, middle-school counselor. Since younger children don't usually leave home by themselves, these boundaries apply to middle and high school students.

Younger children often want to mimic what older kids do. Somehow, the activities of older kids seem more exciting and give young children a chance to feel "grown up." But it's a parent's responsibility to exercise caution, even when kids scream, "I can handle it!" or "Everyone's doing it!" Translated, that could mean anything from attending unchaperoned parties to drinking and using drugs.

When you give children more freedom than they can handle—when you let them reach beyond their years—it's a surefire way for them to fail. To ease the pressure at home, some parents allow younger kids the same freedom given to their older counterparts, but this can place those younger children in danger. They are less mature, more inexperienced, and less capable of handling the unexpected—and certainly no match for the older kids with whom they'll be "hanging out."

Age-based boundaries were a heated topic of conversation with my youngest daughter, Renee. She'd always been an easy child to parent, making good personal choices and earning top grades at school. Then at fourteen, she fell for a young man four years her senior. She wanted to date this new boyfriend, and at every point possible, she reminded us that she was a good kid (which she was) and that Steve was a decent guy (which he was). So why couldn't they date?

It was a tough call. Both teens were all a mom could hope for, and Renee acted mature for her age. I genuinely wanted to please her, to allow her the freedom. But I knew I might be setting her up for a fall. Renee just wasn't old enough; she didn't have the experience to pull off dating someone eighteen years old. Although she often acted older and wiser, there were times she did behave like a fourteen-year-old, or even younger. As a parent, those were the times I needed to remember and be prepared for. As much as I wanted to say yes, I had to say no.

Finally, I told Renee, "Imagine you're standing on a step ladder. As a freshman just starting high school, you're on the bottom rung. Right now, you're doing all of the fun things appropriate for a fourteen-year-old. However, as an eighteen-year-old senior, Steve is at the top of the ladder. He's enjoying all of the freedom, responsibilities, and privileges for a young man his age.

"If you date Steve, where will you end up on the ladder? Is Steve going to be satisfied coming back to the ladder's bottom rung with you? Or will he want to pull you up the ladder to what's appropriate for him?

"Steve will want to pull you up the ladder. Now I know you handle yourself well, but I'm not certain how you'd manage at the top of the ladder. Even though you're responsible, you don't have the experience and maturity that only years can give."

It made her unhappy, but even though Renee couldn't date, we welcomed her friends into our home. As for Steve, he and Renee often saw one another at church and occasionally spent evenings on the porch swing under the watchful eye of her dad and me. And they have remained friends for years. By not allowing Renee to date someone much older, she was able to safely explore the boundaries of appropriate relationships with friends her own age.

Work hard on setting your kids up for success by establishing age-appropriate boundaries.

Boundaries Based on Actions
The second factor that affects children's boundaries is their conduct, particularly as reflected in their per-

sonal workbooks. Did your kids complete their chores? Did they tell you where they're going with friends? Did they obey household rules? By their actions in the past kids determine how many and what kind of responsibilities and privileges they will have in the future.

All children who have slipped into serious trouble will need tight parameters initially. Key behavioral issues that require limited boundaries are drug and alcohol use, sexual promiscuity, truancy from school, running away from home, or other uncontrollable or serious delinquent behavior. These kids need a short rope and high accountability for the special rules that govern their behavior.

Conversely, operating boundaries can be expanded for children who behave well, still keeping in mind what's appropriate for their age level. Key behavioral issues for these kids are completing their daily stuff and obeying household rules.

Because operating boundaries relate to behavior, these parameters will probably expand and contract according to your children's conduct and their move toward maturity. As I explained in the last chapter, when we required Heather to maintain a C average in each of her classes, we rewarded her with the privilege of going out with friends on weekends. After a while, when she consistently brought home the required grade or better, we gave Heather a later curfew and allowed her to ride home in a friend's car after school.

But then one of Heather's teachers called us. She said that Heather was failing Algebra class and had been filling out her own progress reports! Immediately, we pulled in Heather's boundaries and she lost her weekend and after-school privileges.

When it's necessary to pull in their boundaries, it's also tempting to nag your children about their bad behavior. It's important to discuss their bad choices, but repeated harping probably won't change your kids' actions. Focus, instead, on affirming their progress toward better behavior. After the Algebra incident, we focused on Heather's behavioral progress by stating how well she was doing in other areas like completing her daily stuff. We kept reminding her that she could make good choices. And it was wasn't long until, because of her good behavior, we extended Heather's boundaries again.

Knowing Where to Start
After deciding to define boundaries for your kids, it's challenging to decide where to start. These guidelines can help you, as needed, to effectively set and move boundaries.

KNOWING WHERE TO START

- Start with those things that are important.
- Frequently check up on behavior.
- With out-of-control children, leave nothing to chance.
- Express a positive, confirming attitude.
- Increase responsibilities along with privileges.

Start with those things that are important. Especially with troubled children, work diligently on correcting what's out of control and temporarily let everything else go. These issues will vary from household to household and from child to child.

For one family, the daughter staying in school was the key issue, not whether or not she wore safety pins for earrings. One son repeatedly set fire to the grass at school. His mom decided his knuckle-cracking habit was the least of her worries. If one of your children keeps running away, her messy bedroom can take a back seat for a while.

By not trying to correct everything at once, you won't overkill the situation. And you won't risk winning a battle but losing the war, even with children with less troubling problems.

If it's difficult to identify which behaviors to focus on first, try this method. Fold a piece of paper lengthwise. On one half of the paper, list everything you like about this child, including the things he's doing right. On the other half, list the behaviors you dislike. Be very specific. Now set priorities and list your dislikes in order of importance. Then start with the top three or four items on your list of dislikes, while continually reinforcing the good behavior on your list.

Frequently check up on behavior. For out-of-control kids it's especially crucial to leave nothing to chance. Unfortunately, there's no room to short-change this step. It requires a great deal of time, energy, and effort, but you'll obtain an objective measure of their behavior and a tangible tool for arbitration. Also, you'll communicate to the kids that you care enough to stay involved with them.

At this stage, boundary restrictions might include:

■ earlier curfews for evenings out.

■ monitoring school grades and daily attendance.
■ making sure that children are where they said they'd be on evenings out.
■ screening for possible drug use.

When children successfully follow through with their restrictions, they earn or reestablish your trust in them. If they comply with the items on their lists, you can loosen up their boundaries. If they don't measure up, renew their restrictions on a short-term basis. Kids can handle tough restrictions for a week at a time, especially if their conduct determines how tight their restrictions will be the next week.

Express a positive, affirming attitude. When you implement boundaries, your attitude will affect how well they're received. Avoid an "I'm-going-to-get-you" approach. Try to be positive and encouraging. And every time you check and your kids are doing what they're supposed to do, praise them for it. Let them know that their cooperative behavior can be used by them as a bargaining point at arbitration. For example, in one family the son wanted to use the family car. Instead of demanding that privilege, he came to arbitration prepared with examples from his workbook of responsibility and good behavior. His parents, genuinely pleased by his progress and this logical approach, readily agreed to let him use the car.

Also be sure to commend kids when they don't repeat their poor behavior. For instance, chronic runaways leave home for a variety of reasons, but often it's to avoid conflict with their parents. When parents fight with teens who've run away before and the kids don't leave, the affirmation could be, "I'm proud of you. You really showed me a lot of maturity. Instead of running, you're staying and dealing with some tough issues." This type of affirmation validates good choices and reinforces positive behavior.

If children haven't been successful in turning around their behavior, implement the consequences without commenting on the failure. If it's impossible not to comment, say something like, "That wasn't one of your better choices." Remember: look for areas where your kids have made good choices—especially if they have poor success rates—and comment on those.

Increase responsibilities along with privileges. After your children improve their most pressing behavior problems, it's time to expand their boundaries. Still, their lives shouldn't be all privileges and no responsibilities. As you increase their boundaries, you should also expand their responsibilities. To the list of responsibilities for teens you could add eliminating obscene language, accomplishing chores, or showing courtesy to family members. For younger children, you could add completing homework on time and not provoking siblings. This way, you'll create a continuum of personal change, growth, and maturity.

When Heather abandoned her alcohol and drug use—and passed the ninth grade—we expanded into other areas of responsibility. As a sophomore, she not only earned acceptable grades, but she also made her bed in the morning, did her own

laundry, and cleaned up her vocabulary. During that year, a four-letter word cost her five dollars, but she rarely owed us money for any obscenities.

During the four-and-one-half years that we practiced the Parenting Without Pressure program with Heather, her boundaries expanded and contracted many times. But when she entered college, her boundaries were so loose, she was making almost all of her own decisions. Now that's progress!

GUIDELINES TO SAYING YES

I made many mistakes parenting my kids, and one was that I said no too many times. In fact, I restricted so many things that Heather quit listening altogether. Because I desperately wanted her to turn down dangerous activities such as alcohol and drug use, I started working on saying yes to as much as possible.

Peg Ley, a local counselor, helped me determine the requests to which I could say yes. She suggested that parents should say yes as long as the answer is no to some important questions.

SAYING NO CAN MEAN YES

- Is it illegal?
- Is it immoral?
- Is it inappropriate for the child's age?
- Is it going to hurt the child or anybody else?
- Is it something that will make a difference in five years?

At arbitration, a fifteen-year-old boy announced to his mother that he wanted to dye his hair blue. The mom felt horrified, but then she examined the facts. Her son was an honor-roll student who behaved responsibly. After asking herself the five questions, she decided to say yes. In fact, she dyed his hair for him. Although the son hated his dyed hair and soon cut it off, the mother gained lots of credibility with her son.

Does this mean your kids are entitled to blue hair? No. But carefully pick your battles—and say yes to as much as possible, using the questions as a guide.

Each time you say yes, note that in the Anything and Everything Goes section of the workbook. Then when you say no in the future, you'll be prepared when a child yells, "You're not fair!" You can reply, "I understand how you feel, but on March 14th, April 9th, and June 8th, I said yes. However, this time I'm saying no."

ESTABLISHING HOUSEHOLD RULES

With your children's boundaries established, you can then develop household rules. These rules help define the limits of their boundaries and provide day-to-day guidelines for appropriate behavior. Literally, rules are words kids can live by.

Here's how it works. If a boundary requires your children to be home by dinner time on school nights, the rule can be: "Please be home by 6 o'clock on school nights so you can wash up and set the table for dinner at 6:30." This rule expresses the exact parameters of the curfew and the parents' expectations.

This rule will work fine for kids who generally comply and stay within their operating boundaries. But if a child frequently ignores the rules,

ESTABLISHING HOUSEHOLD RULES

- Let the kids help.
- Be specific about the rules and consequences.
- Explain the necessity of each rule.
- When applying the rules, be consistent and fair.
- Start with rules you can enforce.
- Always include a disobeying rule.

you'll want to add a consequence: "If you're not home by 6 o'clock—and you haven't called to explain that it's an emergency—you'll lose your phone privileges for that night." When behaviors need modification, rules need stated consequences.

However, there's more to household rules than just writing words on paper. It's a process that considers the needs and feelings of both the parents and the kids, and it requires time, work, and patience to write out and enforce them. As you develop your household rules, keep the following guidelines in mind.

Let the kids help. This communicates that you want to be fair and that you care about their feelings. Also, when kids have the opportunity to participate in making the rules and consequences, they are much more likely to cooperate with them. It's hard to argue with something they've had a part in formulating.

One parent said her son continually left the radio at maximum volume after driving the car. Because she was continually being blasted out of the front seat, she brought this up for discussion at arbitration. Her son agreed to try to remember to turn down the radio after using the car and suggested he'd wash and wax it if he forgot.

Although it is important that children be allowed to participate in the rule writing, there will be times when parents cannot compromise; for example, allowing a child to use alcohol or drugs.

Be specific about the rules and consequences. Never deal in generalities. A rule that says, "Please be home on time or you'll be in trouble" only leads to arguments. It's better to write, "You must be home and inside by 12:00 p.m. or your curfew for the next date will be 11:00 p.m."

Very quickly, kids will use the workbook to their advantage. They'll work overtime at finding loopholes. This happened to a dad who hadn't been specific about his son's curfew. When he walked through the door at 1:00 a.m., the father angrily announced to his son, "You're an hour past your curfew!" His son looked surprised.

"But Dad," he said, "I was home at midnight. I was outside talking to my friends!"

You can eliminate problems like this by being specific.

Explain the necessity of each rule. When a child asks why, it's no longer acceptable to say, "Because I said so! That's why!" Take the time to explain the rationale behind household rules. This will help children clearly understand the necessity for the specific restrictions or rules.

A single mother of a fourteen-year-old boy shared this household rule and the necessity behind it: "No swimming in the backyard pool when an adult is not home." She explained to him that this was a safety issue. In case of an emergency, a responsible adult might be needed.

Unfortunately, some people must control every aspect of their children's lives, and consequently, end up with rules, rules, rules. Then they're surprised when their kids disobey. If you create too many rules or unnecessary rules, your kids probably won't comply, just to get some breathing space.

When applying the rules, be consistent and fair. As I mentioned earlier, consistency is the key to a parenting program's success. But it's your fairness that will win over kids more than anything else. Fairness includes giving your children "the benefit of the doubt" as much as possible.

You can determine how much leeway to give by consulting the children's notebooks. For example, a child arrives home twenty-five minutes late and says his friend's car had a flat tire. If his workbook reflects that normally he's been coming home on time, chances are he's telling you the truth. You can let him off the hook. On the other hand, if he's had several questionable incidences in the last month or has been late frequently, there's probably reason to doubt the alibi. You'll need to enforce the consequence.

When you give your children the benefit of the doubt, be sure to note it in the Anything and Everything Goes section of their workbooks. If at some point someone screams that you're not fair, again, you'll have a record of the times you've been understanding.

Start with rules you can enforce. Otherwise, kids will manipulate their way out of the consequences. I dealt with this problem when Heather kept smoking despite my rule that she should not. This habit turned into a heated issue at our house. When Heather went out with friends, she often smelled like smoke when she returned home. In an outrage, I'd accuse her of smoking and, of course, she'd deny it and the argument was on!

In reality, I couldn't prove that Heather had been smoking, even though I felt certain about it. Therefore, I changed the household rule about smoking. At arbitration, I revised the rule to say, "You may not smoke in my presence or in our home. If I find cigarettes in your possession, I will throw them out and deduct their cost from your next week's allowance." I revised the rule so Heather would learn that broken rules have consequences; she couldn't disobey and get away with it. I created a rule I could enforce.

Always include a disobeying rule. This rule takes care of willful, defiant behavior for which there is no rule. Because many times this is going to be a judgment call on the part of the parent, this is the most subjective aspect of the workbook.

A week after Heather's grandfather purchased a new Cutlass Supreme, he left town on business for two weeks. He didn't want to leave the car unattended in his driveway, so he parked it at our house for safekeeping. Imagine my reaction when Heather took the car, loaded with friends, to the beach for several hours. We didn't have a rule that said Heather couldn't take her grandfather's car to the beach. But without a doubt, she knew she'd committed

an infraction. That's when I fell back on the disobeying rule.

Heather's disobeying rule said, "Any act of willful disobedience will result in Heather being grounded until the next arbitration. At that arbitration, we will discuss if an additional consequence should be added." Heather's consequence? Since we'd just had an arbitration, she was grounded for a week. At the next arbitration, we decided Heather would lose her phone and television privileges for the next two weeks and write a letter of apology to her grandfather.

PULLING IT TOGETHER

When Herb and I established boundaries and rules for our daughters, we learned some timeless principles helpful for pulling everything together. They're from the best-selling book *The Strong Willed Child*, by Dr. James Dobson.[1] I've taught these ideas at the Parenting Without Pressure workshops.

PULLING IT TOGETHER

- Define the boundaries before they're enforced.
- When defiantly challenged, respond with confident decisiveness.
- Distinguish between willful defiance and childish irresponsibility.
- Reassure and teach your children after a confrontation.
- Avoid impossible demands.
- Let love be your guide.

"Define the Boundaries Before They're Enforced

Always establish reasonable expectations and boundaries in advance. Children should know what's expected of them before they're responsible for it. If you haven't defined it, don't enforce it."

Before I understood this guideline, I'd sometimes blame Heather for breaking a rule when we had never clearly defined the rule or its consequence. How unfair for her! When this happened—and it wasn't a case of willful, defiant behavior— I apologized. Then I noted what Heather had done in the Anything and Everything Goes section and discussed it with Heather at the next arbitration.

"When Defiantly Challenged, Respond with Confident Decisiveness

There's nothing more destructive to parental leadership than for a mother or father to disintegrate during a struggle. Keep your emotions under control."

My friend Dave cued me to the effectiveness of responding decisively. Several years ago he was badly injured in a very serious automobile accident. Dave said his most vivid memory and the most important factor to which he attributed his survival was the paramedic who never left his side. The calm manner with which the paramedic spoke and the decisive way he took charge told Dave he was going to make it. Later, when I found myself in a crisis situation with Heather where things normally escalated out of control, I tried this technique. It worked! From then on, the more out of control Heather was, the more decisive my speech was and the softer my voice became.

This produced a calming and reassuring effect that allowed Heather to calm down without feeling she was giving up control. Also, by utilizing this technique with her, she learned to appropriately cope with her anger and deal with stressful situations.

"Distinguish Between Willful Defiance and Childish Irresponsibility

Before you discipline your children, determine their intent behind the mistakes. Willful defiance is deliberate disobedience—when children know what parents expect from them and do the opposite. This could include running away when called, screaming insults, and other acts of outright disobedience. Kids know when they're wrong and wait to see what their parents will do about it." For willful, defiant behavior, make use of the disobeying rule.

As a young teenager, Renee dressed for school in a T-shirt that I felt was inappropriate. I said, "Renee, that's an interesting shirt, but it's not suitable for school. Please go change your clothes." And she did. But after she gathered her lunch, book bag, and clarinet and left for school, I had nagging doubts about the status of the T-shirt. After canceling several appointments for that morning, I drove to Renee's school and asked to see her. I told the office staff not to tell her I was there, but just to request that she come to the office. You can imagine Renee's face when she walked into the office wearing the T-shirt.

Renee's disobeying rule said that any willful act of disobedience would result in extra chores—my choice, not hers. Because Renee was an academically strong student, I checked her out of school. On the way home, we stopped at a nursery where I asked the attendant to fill the car's trunk with mulch. Arriving at home, I told Renee to weed and mulch anything that resembled a flower bed. She'd been defiant and I wanted the consequence to be tough.

"In contrast, childish irresponsibility results from forgetfulness, accidents, inattentiveness, intolerance, or immaturity." A mom from one of my workshops related this example of childish irresponsibility. After spending a day moving into their new home, the family's teenage daughter took a break to polish her nails. As she sat on the new white couch in a formal living room with matching carpeting and drapes, the daughter vigorously shook the red nail polish bottle. Somehow the top of the bottle flew off and polish spread on the wall, drapes, sofa, and carpet. Willful, defiant behavior? No. Just a kid acting like a kid.

"Reassure and Teach Your Children After a Confrontation"

Because Heather had become a master at giving the responsibility for her behavior to everyone else in the family, Dr. David Parker, our psychologist, taught us this debriefing technique. This easy technique involves asking the questions why, what, and how:

1. *Why* did you lose this privilege?

2. *What* will happen if you make that choice again?

3. *How* can you do it differently in the future?

Heather was required to answer the questions correctly before we would reinstate whatever she had lost as a consequence.

For example, Heather was not allowed to talk on the phone after 10:00 p.m. To do so resulted in losing the phone for a day. And when she lost the phone because she had not complied with the rule, she was required to answer the above questions before the privilege was returned.

1. Why did you lose your phone?

"I lost my phone because I was using it after 10:00 p.m."

2. What will happen if you talk on the phone after hours again?

"I will lose the phone for a day."

3. How can you do it differently in the future?

"I will not talk on the phone after 10:00 p.m."

Upon completing this debriefing technique, there was not a doubt that Heather clearly understood the rule, what the consequence was for breaking the rule, and more important, how she could do it differently the next time.

"Avoid Impossible Demands

Parents should understand their children's limitations and adjust their expectations accordingly." For example, don't expect an eight-year-old child with ADHD (attention deficit disorder with hyperactivity) to sit quietly for two hours. Or don't leave a fifteen-year-old who struggles with basic rules home alone for the weekend.

"Let Love Be Your Guide

A relationship characterized by genuine love and affection will be a healthy one, even though parental mistakes are inevitable." As Herb and I struggled initially with Heather's behavior, we made many parenting mistakes. But what kept the doors of communication open was the unconditional love she felt and the dignity and respect with which she was treated.

HOMEWORK FOR PARENTS

Before you write household rules for your children, ask yourself:

1. What are my motives for establishing rules?

2. What has been my attitude about rules in the past?

3. How might I need to change my attitude or actions?

4. What difficulties will I encounter while establishing these rules?

5. What can I do to resolve these difficulties?

6. When formulating my children's rules, in what areas can I make compromises?

CHAPTER FOUR

What They Do Is What They Get
Creating real consequences and incentives.

The beautiful antique oak coffee table was one of her most prized possessions. It had belonged to her maternal grandmother and recently, when her mother died, her father gave it to her. Consequently, you can imagine her horror when she discovered the huge scratch gouged across its top. Her young teenage son carelessly caused it when he used the table as a stand for his video game. His mother was devastated and furious. Because she wanted him to experience the pain of having something he valued damaged, she took a nail and scraped his skateboard. What did she accomplish in this? Did she teach him anything about respect for another's property or restitution?

Unfortunately, some parents see consequences only as punishment for children's misbehavior. And tragically, the parental motive of teaching responsibility and appropriate behavior gets lost in satisfying their need for power, control, and revenge. Sound far-fetched? How many times have you heard a parent say, "When I say jump, my kids ask how high!" Do you know of a parent whose immediate response to every request is "No!" Have you heard stories about people who, like the parent mentioned above, retaliate?

Don't let any of that be true for you. Your motive for implementing consequences should be to deter, change, modify, or reinforce your children's behavior. This will encourage learning and cooperation between you and them. And it teaches the important distinction between acts of "discipline" and "punishment."

Discipline derives from the root word *disciple* and it means "to teach." It's a positive, pro-active approach that focuses on teaching children appropriate behavior. On the other hand, punishment means "to chastise or correct." It negatively addresses misbehavior after it's occurred. Parents who confuse these two concepts apply a lot of punishment with little or no discipline—and everyone's unhappy. The good news is that the more you properly discipline children, the less you'll need to punish them. And it begins with the principle of "cause and effect."

"Cause and effect" as it applies to discipline means that every time your children don't follow their rules, specific consequences result—and without punitive comments from you. To this principle, you can add the dimension of incentives. These are rewards for following rules, and

they add a positive dimension to the discipline process.

This parenting technique, called behavior modification, simply rewards desired behavior and discourages undesirable behavior. This results in a behavioral change that can be immediate and lasting when coupled with helping children intrinsically identify the wonderful feeling of accomplishment and doing things right.

For example, a dad I know successfully used incentives with his fifteen-year-old son who frequently skipped school. This boy didn't attend classes for more than two weeks without missing a day. The father and son fought continually, especially about the son's driving privileges, which were nonexistent because of the truancies. The family seemed locked in a conflict it couldn't resolve.

Fortunately, the dad eventually stepped back and identified the behavior he desired from his son: He desperately wanted the teen to stay in school. After this, he consid-

ered what it would take to accomplish his goal and utilized the cause-and-effect approach. At arbitration, he and his wife established this rule: "You must attend all of your classes at school every day. If you skip any classes during the week, you will be grounded for the entire next week, including the weekend. If, however, you attend all of your classes every day for two weeks, you can get your learner's permit. For every day after the two weeks that you attend all of your classes, we will give you an hour's practice driving time on the weekend." Additionally, his dad provided plenty of praise, encouragement, and appreciation, and focused daily on his son's success.

When I last talked to his parents, the son hadn't skipped school in a month and was turning around his academic performance. He'd also obtained his driver's license. With the cause-effect-incentive approach to consequences, you can modify your children's behavior, give them real incentive to change, and help them identify the feeling of successfully doing things well.

DIFFERENT TYPES
OF CONSEQUENCES

Rudolf Dreikurs, a highly respected child psychiatrist, developed the concept of natural and logical consequences.[1] Both of these are very effective and frequently utilized with behavior modification or the cause-effect-incentive parenting approach.

A natural consequence is one that takes place with no parental intervention; for example, a child going hungry after forgetting to take her lunch to school. Logical consequences require parental intervention and are related to the behavior; for example, if a child does not put his bike in the garage at night, he will not be able to ride it the next day.

Parents also can utilize a child's leverage points when determining consequences. A leverage point is anything a child holds dear, really wants, or can't stand to lose. Because leverage points vary from child to child, consequences for the same rule may vary among children. A working consequence for not completing daily stuff by a specific time might be the loss of the phone for one child and the loss of the television for another.

Often what works best are logical consequences that utilize a child's leverage points.

THREE SIMPLE CONSEQUENCE COMPONENTS

If possible, consider these three components when formulating consequences. The first involves something the child values. Parents can determine those things simply by identifying a child's leverage points. Ask yourself: "Where does he spend his time?" "What does he like to do?" "What does he value?" One child loved to play with friends after school. Hence, losing that privilege would make an excellent consequence.

Teaching is also an important consequence component. An excellent way to accomplish this is by using the debriefing technique explained on page 47. Another effective teaching method is requiring kids to write short essays related to the problem behavior. One mom had her daughter, who had purchased a

---

THREE SIMPLE CONSEQUENCE COMPONENTS

1. Loss of something the child values.
2. Teaching what's right.
3. Restitution.

---

fake ID, research and document the legal ramifications of possessing fake identification. She then required her daughter to have five friends read and sign the document. (The mother felt certain that these friends also had fake IDs.)

The final component is restitution. Children can learn at an early age that whenever it's possible, they should right a wrong. That means they should make restitution to the person they've hurt or for what they've damaged or destroyed. Recently when a group of youngsters vandalized a local baseball dugout, as part of the consequence for their actions, they were required to clean, repair, and paint the dugout.

Other Guidelines for Consequences

Less is better: Keep consequences as small as possible. When using consequences, your goal is to modify or change children's behavior. If a little consequence (losing the phone for an evening) accomplishes that, use it. Add to a small consequence (losing the phone *plus* losing the TV for an evening) or use a bigger consequence (being grounded for the weekend) only when the behavior warrants it.

Keep consequences short-term. If you apply short-term consequences, children see an end to them and an opportunity to behave differently the next time. If a child loses the phone for a day because her daily stuff wasn't completed, she can regain it tomorrow simply by doing her chores. When a teen gets grounded because he didn't earn a 2.0 grade point average for the week, he knows it's only for the weekend. Next week he can improve his grades and keep his privileges. When kids don't see an end to the consequence or a way they can win, they quickly shut down and quit trying.

Consequences and behavior should correspond. A consequence should correspond to the transgression. Therefore, decide on consequences by determining intent first. A child who totally disregarded family rules should have a tougher consequence than one who acted immaturely or irresponsibly.

OTHER GUIDELINES FOR CONSEQUENCES

- Less is better: Keep consequences as small as possible.
- Keep consequences short-term.
- A consequence should correspond to the transgression.

Also, consequences usually won't fit behaviors if you're angry when you establish them. Instead, take time to cool off and create the consequences at an arbitration meeting. It will give you the opportunity to examine your children's behavior and, with their help, choose appropriate consequences.

AVOIDING THE TRAPS

As mentioned in chapter 2, after household rules and consequences have been established at arbitration,

parents can easily fall into two traps. They can discuss the consequence after the rule is broken, which will usually lead to an argument; or they can simply not follow through with the consequence.

Children learn quickly how to manipulate their way out of consequences. Some other tactics include:

- Throwing a tantrum: nagging, begging, and screaming relentlessly. "I can't believe you're so mean! Why do you treat me this way? You're unfair!"
- Promising to behave: swearing to never repeat the behavior. "I'm sorry! I'll never, ever do it again."
- Threatening to misbehave: promising drastic action to avoid the consequences and to punish you. "If you don't let me attend that concert, I'll run away!"
- Reforming immediately: doing whatever they think is necessary—or even unnecessary—to please you. This tactic works the best because it inspires warm feelings and makes it tough to apply consequences. "Mom, I just cleaned my room and now I'm taking the dog out for a walk."
- Attacking when you're down: waiting until you're physically tired and mentally exhausted, then hitting with a verbal vengeance. "Why can't you be like Jennifer's parents? They aren't mean to her. I hate you!"
- Withdrawing love: pulling away and punishing you with silence or absence. "I'm going to go live with Dad. He appreciates me more than you do!"

■ Spreading the guilt: making you feel guilty or sorry because of a special problem such as a physical handicap or a broken home or an addicted parent. "If you weren't divorced, I wouldn't be so messed up!"
■ Blaming the parent: placing the responsibility for the action on the parent. "If you bought me an alarm clock I could hear, I wouldn't miss the school bus."

When it's time to apply consequences, hang on through the manipulation. By allowing children to weasel their way out of consequences, you'll communicate that they don't have to be accountable for their actions. You could also allow them to set an unhealthy pattern of irresponsibility for the rest of their lives.

CONSEQUENCES THAT COUNT

Some parents have a difficult time determining exactly what they can and cannot use as consequences. What they usually hear from a child is, "You can't take that. I bought it with my own money," or "You can't take my car. Dad bought it for me." Parents, yes you can take things away. In addition to a great deal of dignity and respect, you owe your children only four things.

THINGS PARENTS MUST
GIVE THEIR CHILDREN

■ A roof over their heads
■ Three healthy meals a day
■ Clothing to wear
■ Unconditional love—a great deal of unconditional love

When you choose consequences, you might want to begin with those that other parents have administered successfully. These are consequences that have worked for me and for parents from the Parenting Without Pressure workshops.

■ Removing the televisions, CD players, or telephones from the house. More than once I've traveled around town with the television in the trunk of my car. If you want to use the telephone, screen the kids' incoming calls with an answering machine. And if the family wants to watch TV, send the child who lost that privilege to her room.
■ Withholding favorite items. Things like bicycles, skate boards, and video games can be taken away. One mom was surprised at the cooperation she received from her daughter by removing her cream rinse!
■ Taking away the allowance or lunch money. Does this mean your children go without lunch? Absolutely not. Buy large jars of peanut butter and jam, a loaf of bread and lots of brown bags. And let the kids make the sandwiches.
■ Charging money for four-letter words. Also charge money for unkind statements directed at siblings.
■ Writing sentences for four-letter words. Require a child to write, "I will not use profanity" 100 to 200 times.
■ Writing an essay from 200 to 500 words long to explain the reason behind a specific improper behavior. This is

extremely effective for children who have difficulty verbalizing.

■ Assigning extra work around the house. This can include washing all the windows and screens, cleaning out kitchen cabinets or closets, and yard work.

■ Grounding children to their bedrooms, the house, or yard for a day, weekend, or week.

■ Delivering a lecture at arbitration. The topic is yours to choose and it can deal with anything from the importance of getting an education and being honest to the difficulty caused by being sexually active or doing drugs.

■ Walking to or from school. If they chronically miss the bus, kids can walk to school. If the school is in a rough area, map out a safe route to walk or follow the kids in the car. If children chronically get school detentions, let them walk home. (A child should walk to or from school only if it is safe.) Some schools have early-morning detentions. That means arriving at school by 6:00 a.m. This might be rough on you, but it's very effective for kids.

■ Stopping transportation to an enoyable activity such as a movie or skating. Heather learned quickly that she must treat me respectfully if she wanted me to provide transportation for a movie with her friends.

■ Using a driver's license as a bargaining tool. A parent's signature is required for an adolescent to obtain a driver's license. You can also take away a teenager's license.

Again, use incentives whenever possible and make them big enough so youngsters will want to cooperate. Rather than a win-lose approach, give everyone a chance to win. And always remember to discuss the consequences with children prior to using them. They have the right to know what to expect before, not after, the fact.

THE MAGIC OF INCENTIVES

Positive consequences or incentives are intrinsic and extrinsic rewards that reinforce or motivate children toward good behavior. Intrinsic rewards help motivate children from within, teaching them to look inside themselves for good behavior. Extrinsic rewards grant children material rewards or privileges, motivating them to work toward things they'd like to obtain.

An example of an intrinsic reward is praise. Comments such as, "I noticed how well you handled yourself when you became angry"

THE MAGIC OF INCENTIVES

Intrinsic Rewards	Extrinsic Rewards
Praise	Money
Appreciation	Privileges
Encouragements	Material items

can get a lot of mileage and cause the child to want to repeat the behavior. Encouragement and appreciation are other intrinsic rewards.

An example of an extrinsic reward is an incentive such as money. You might tell a child that if he completes all the daily stuff for a week, you'll double that week's allowance. Other extrinsic rewards include special privileges and material things.

Because intrinsic rewards work much better and the results are longer lasting, that's what a parent wants to use most of the time. It's most important that in addition to praise, encouragement, and appreciation you always help a child develop competency in her ability to make good choices and have control over her behavior.

Extrinsic rewards are terrific motivators and work especially well with challenging or noncompliant children. However, always use extrinsic rewards combined with intrinsic rewards.

When to Use Incentives

Some parents have a difficult time with incentives because they consider them bribes. But there is a big difference between the two. Bribes are used to buy good behavior; incentives are used to teach appropriate behavior.

Incentives are best used when:

Rewarding very good (specific) behavior. For instance, your twin girls sat quietly for hours and politely listened to Great Aunt Gertrude's repeated stories about her childhood.

Reinforcing children struggling with a particular behavior. It's helpful to reinforce a new behavior a child is struggling to learn. For example, when a boy channels his anger at a punching bag rather than a person, the time is ripe for an incentive.

WHEN TO USE INCENTIVES

1. Rewarding a very good (specific) behavior.
2. Reinforcing children struggling with a particular behavior.
3. Nothing else is working.

Nothing else is working. When you are at a lose/lose stage, you can start over by adding incentives and creating a win/win situation. Recently a couple shared that for months their rebellious daughter had lost all privileges because of her refusal to comply with any rules. In a tug of war, they were adding on the consequences and she was refusing to budge. Because she had "shut down" completely, her parents wisely decided to start over with a clean slate. Only this time they gave her a reason to cooperate by making it a win/win situation.

If she obeyed the rules for two weeks, she could have her own phone line. And for each week she complied after that, she would earn use of it for the following week. As she followed the rules (initially because she wanted to use the phone), her parents diligently worked on helping her grasp the tremendous feeling of doing things right! And as her success rate grew, so did her ability to see herself as a kid you could count on!

A quick tip: Always reward incentives after the fact, never before. And because of shorter attention spans,

SETTING UP TOKEN ECONOMIES

One great method for applying incentives is handing out tokens that kids can cash in for their rewards. Poker chips make excellent tokens, but if you have more than one child, assign each one a different color chip. When you determine the worth of each token, always use the children's ages and the difficulty of the behavior. Also, be realistic about what your family can afford if tokens are to be cashed in for material items. And remember, to participate is to have ownership in something. Therefore, allow the children to have as much input as possible.

Token economies help increase good behavior. Try these ways to reward your children when they have earned the number of tokens that you think each one is worth.

For younger children, ages 6-12:
- A later bedtime
- Playing a special game
- An extra story before bed
- Eating at a favorite restaurant
- Buying a new toy
- Going to a movie with friends
- Bowling with friends
- Having a sleep-over party
- Biking with mom or dad

For older children, ages 13-18:
- Buying new clothes
- Dating privileges
- Haircuts or permanents
- A trip to the beach
- A new radio or CD player
- A private phone
- Getting a part-time job
- An extended curfew
- Tapes or compact discs
- A driver's license
- Additional makeup
- Use of the family car
- New shoes (their choice)
- Redecorating a bedroom
- Additional allowance money

the younger the child, the sooner he should receive the reward.

TOUGH CONSEQUENCES FOR TOUGH KIDS

Noncompliant youngsters usually fall into two categories. They may feel they have already lost everything and are now saying, "I don't care what you do." And they mean it. Or they respond to parental authority with, "You and what army is going to make me?"

Noncompliant youngsters can be tough and challenging. For one rea-son, oppositional defiant behavior, alcohol and drug abuse, and depression are common with many noncompliant children. Parents struggling with these children should seek counseling. A competent therapist can help identify and treat emotional problems a child might be experiencing. It's also helpful to have a better understanding of noncompliant youngsters.

When a child feels he has nothing to lose, he has no reason to cooperate. This often results when a parent has taken everything from the child as consequences for breaking rules so the child simply has shut down. Sadly, many of these kids also feel they have nothing to lose outside the home. They see themselves with little hope and little or no future.

As tough as they seem, these kids still long for parental approval. Unfortunately, they often perceive parental frustration and anger as rejection, and that adds to their "you-don't-care-so-why-should-I" feeling. As parents diligently work on the issue of compliance, they should dismantle the hostility in the home by creating an atmosphere for cooperation. By utilizing the cause-effect-incentive approach, they can correct negative behavior while shifting their focus to what the child is doing right.

Often noncompliant children have bottomed out with their self-esteem. Consequently, they will go to any lengths to be accepted by their peers. It is vitally important, therefore, that parents help enhance their self-esteem and make sure these kids feel accepted at home.

Tough Choices
Unfortunately, sometimes a parent has no other choice but to implement tough consequences. This may mean involving the police and/or juvenile authorities. Legally, parents can protect themselves and their property, and sometimes it takes drastic steps for a youngster to understand this.

Carefully explain the following consequences at arbitration. And always conclude with this statement: "I don't want to (whatever the consequence is), and I'm sure you don't want me to either. However, it will be

---

TOUGH KIDS

1. They feel they have nothing to lose.
2. They long for parental approval.
3. Many are from families involved in a power struggle that only adds to a child's feelings of rejection.
4. Noncompliant kids usually suffer from poor self-esteem.
5. They are probably using alcohol and/or drugs, and may be dependent on them.

---

a choice that you make. Please don't (break whatever the rule is)."

1. Remove the bedroom door. Adolescents thrive on privacy, so this can be an eye-opening experience.

2. Remove the bedroom furniture, including dressers, end tables, and bed frames, so that the only thing left is a mattress on the floor. This consequence should be used only when you have exhausted everything else.

3. If your child threatens to run away, inform her at arbitration that the street is a dangerous place and she may not run. If she chooses to do so, then you should do the following immediately:

 a. Notify the police and report her missing.
 b. Contact every missing children's agency in your state and provide them with a recent photograph.
 c. Tell her friends' parents that your child does not have permission to be any place other than home, and if she is

staying there against your wishes, you will press charges. (Usually kids who run away stay with friends.)
d. Remove all the furniture from her bedroom and put her personal things in storage. Leave them there for a week after she returns.

4. If a youngster is using either alcohol or drugs, require random drug screenings and seek counseling. If within a six-to-eight-week period, the drug screenings are not negative, residential treatment might be necessary for the child. (Alcohol is difficult to catch on a drug screening, so a parent will have to watch carefully for signs of alcohol use.)

5. If a child threatens you, strikes you, steals from you, or "trashes" your home and you feel that his conduct is the result of unusual circumstances, seek immediate crisis counseling.

A parent can press criminal charges against a child if the child threatens a parent's safety, strikes him, steals from him, or trashes the home. If the police officer refuses to take a report, request his name and badge number and ask for his immediate supervisor's name. Report him and ask his supervisor to file the charge. If that is not successful, call the officer complaint line. Explain that a police officer and his supervisor would not press charges even though you felt threatened. Again state that you want to file charges.

The worst thing a parent can do is file the charges and then drop them. Be sure you can follow through before you file charges.

6. If a child is on community control or non-secure detention, make an appointment to see his caseworker. Establish in writing what he is prepared to do if the child is abusive to a parent, or violates his probation, or doesn't comply with the rules. If the child's behavior makes it necessary, call his caseworker and insist he follow through with the child's sanctions. Also ask his caseworker to notify the judge and ask that a pickup order be issued. Parents should always maintain detailed notes on the child's behavior and their juvenile justice/court documentation.

7. If the child is eighteen or older and chronically acts up, tell him to leave. Because juvenile laws have changed drastically in the past few years, a parent may want to talk to an attorney specializing in juvenile law. Names of attorneys can be obtained from the Bar Association Referral Service.

The best consequence is the natural consequence. As much as possible, parents should allow the natural consequences for behavior to occur without interference. Allowing your child to experience the real world can be a real eye-opening experience for him. Every out-of-control child who thinks rules apply to everyone but him should have to bail himself out of jail, get fired for chronically showing up late for work, pay fines for speeding tickets, have charges filed when he puts his foot through a wall, or be held in contempt of court for failure to comply with the rules. By allowing a child to reap the consequences of his own behavior, parents teach him that he is responsible for his choices. They show him that they refuse to take on his responsibilities.

Finally, it is important to remember that not all consequences are negative. Reward good behavior or even bad behavior when it is not repeated.

HOMEWORK FOR PARENTS

Before you start arbitrations with your kids (see next chapter), think through the following things for each child.

1. What exactly do I want to accomplish?

2. Where should each child's operating boundaries be?

3. With which specific behavioral areas should I begin?

4. Formulate each child's first few basic rules. Be very specific and avoid loopholes.

5. Determine each child's leverage points. Formulate several consequences, again avoiding loopholes.

6. Establish specific things that can be utilized as incentives.

CHAPTER FIVE

Talking Down a Storm

Fostering open arbitration and communication.

When my daughter Renee was a sixth grader, more than anything else, she wanted to attend a Valentine's Day dance at a middle school. More than anything, I didn't want her to go. She was only eleven years old. The dance was at night. The school was in a rough area. I'm really old fashioned. She was only eleven years old! Every day Renee brought up the dance. And every day I reminded her that I wanted to talk about it, but she needed to save it for arbitration.

When that day arrived, Renee's first question was, "Can we discuss the dance now?" I started by defining the problem. She wanted to attend a dance about which I felt very uncomfortable, and I explained the reasons why. Renee didn't say much until it was her turn to talk. Then she calmly explained that I didn't know much about dances today; that they're different than the social events I attended years ago. Then she did something I'll never forget. Renee politely handed me a list of names and phone numbers of people associated with the school. The principal, guidance counselors, teachers—they were all on her list.

"Mom," she said, "please call these people this week and ask them about the dance. Then at arbitration next week, let's discuss it again."

As I sat there with my mouth open, I realized Renee had beaten me at my own game. She'd dealt with the facts and thought them through, something I'd wanted her to learn to do. I had no choice but to do my homework and call the people on the list. And Renee was right: I didn't know much about the dance.

The next week at arbitration, Renee and I brainstormed the different options and chose a solution we both could live with. She'd go to the dance and I would volunteer as a chaperone. However, while I was at the dance, Renee wanted me to fade into the background and not embarrass her. I was not to wave at her or her friends, give her any eye contact or acknowledge her presence in any way. I honored Renee's requests that night. I watched from a distance and sold lots of drinks and popcorn.

WHAT ARBITRATION IS

Renee's school dance episode represented arbitration at its best. We held our meetings on a weekly basis. We saved our arguments until the meetings. We calmly discussed a point of disagreement. We developed a compromise that we could both live with. We entered the agreement in her workbook. We stuck to it.

Granted, this isn't the way all arbitrations go, especially when you're getting started. But it's a goal to strive for—getting both sides to calmly discuss and resolve a problem into a win/win situation.

As I said in chapter 2, arbitration should take place when everyone's rested and feeling good. Saturday mornings work best for my family. However, you might consider one-to-one meetings with your children for several possible reasons: busy schedules make it difficult getting the whole family together at a specific time; individual kids request privacy; or you're a single parent and the kids have a tendency to gang up on you.

The important thing is to establish a set time and place for arbitration, to give it priority and to stress its importance. It often works well to conduct arbitration at the kitchen or dining room table. Kids stay focused more easily if they're sitting in chairs, looking at their parents. Also, you can stress the importance of arbitration by turning off the television, radio, and CD player, and letting the answering machine pick up phone calls.

It's also important to be consistent in having arbitrations, especially when there are no heavy-duty items to discuss. In addition to resolving conflicts, arbitration can also prevent them. It's an excellent pressure valve, allowing parents and children to address small issues before they grow into big problems. This pressure-valve aspect functions when you meet regularly, no matter the circumstances.

WHAT ARBITRATION IS NOT!

Arbitration is not the only time families communicate. Be available and never miss an opportunity to talk with your children. Never use arbitration as a substitution for conversation at meal times. Family meals should be enjoyable and free of hassles. And don't use arbitration as an emotional dumping ground for you and your spouse. When emotions such as anger and frustration go unchecked, it is easy to blame all the household problems on a challenging youngster. Take care of your emotional baggage before arbitration.

WHAT ARBITRATION CAN DO FOR YOUR FAMILY

Weekly meetings. A workbook for each child. Negotiating rules and boundaries. At first, family arbitrations sound like a lot of work. However, if you keep at it, arbitrations will easily turn into a regular family routine that you and your kids appreciate. Here's what arbitration can do for you and your family.

Eliminates Everyday Skirmishes

Arbitration is the only time during the week that you discuss confrontational issues and the workbook's contents. It's also the only time you establish rules and renegotiate boundaries. With these guidelines in place, the kids can't force you into quick decisions or badger you into caving in. Rather, you can clearly think through issues without making mistakes that cause you to backtrack later. This is especially helpful during a family crisis. Arbitration provides a safe setting to discuss important problems without escalating the situation. And it eliminates repeated discussions about the same problems.

Improves Your Home's Emotional Atmosphere

Arbitration is the only time during the week that you accept the challenge to do battle. Translated, this means arbitration is the only time

you argue with your children about confrontational issues. The rest of the week you work at getting along with each other.

Does this mean children automatically follow through with consequences and wait until arbitration to complain about issues? Unfortunately, no. As parents, most of us have allowed kids to hook us into arguments by ranting and raving. Inadvertently, we've taught our kids that if they nag long enough, we will cave in and they'll win.

With an established arbitration time, you can reteach kids that "I say what I mean and mean what I say" will always apply. Your response to the nagging can be, "I can see that you're really upset and I'm sorry. But we will discuss it at arbitration." This may prove difficult initially because in many homes the destructive pattern of daily warfare has long been established. However, a change can be accomplished if parents remember that it takes two to have an argument.

Establishes Routine Accountability

Some kids can be masters of deception, and their parents never feel sure of what they're doing. A weekly arbitration can eliminate this uncertainty when you and your kids sit down and examine the facts. That leaves no room for surprises. When I felt uncomfortable about a situation with Heather and asked for an explanation, she sometimes replied, "Later, Mom. I gotta go!" At arbitration, she couldn't go anywhere and I'd ask for a detailed explanation. We stayed at the table until she answered satisfactorily.

Builds a Constructive Avenue of Communication

In a way, arbitration can help you talk down storms rather than stir them up. It's an excellent time for family members to clear the air and say what's on their minds. Not only can the kids work out disagreements with you, but siblings can resolve differences with each other. This type of constructive yet emotional outlet can help family members understand each other better and tear down mounting barriers among them.

For two years, Heather used arbitration to talk to Herb and me about how miserable she felt. We gave her this weekly platform because she needed to express her feelings and know that we'd heard her. Hence we were able to communicate our interest, love, and concern, and validate her feelings of self-worth.

The added bonus in arbitration is that by eliminating daily fighting, providing for accountability, and opening lines of communication, it allows families to make the home a safe and positive place for everybody!

BEFORE STARTING ARBITRATION

Once you've decided to add regular arbitrations to your family life, there are a few things you need to know before you begin. The first is that you might be unpopular for awhile, especially with kids who've grown up without family meetings and who are used to a loosely structured environment. As with enforcing consequences, you'll need to hang on through the initial complaints and manipulations, especially from older children. They might need an adjustment period, and their responses to arbitration will vary as much as their personalities.

Next, be sure that your family's authority figures are operating as a united front. Parenting styles are diverse, and often adults don't agree on the basics. In my family, Herb's style was, in my opinion, very permissive. I'd joke that if the kids wanted to build a bonfire in the family room, he'd go get the matches.

> **BEFORE STARTING ARBITRATION**
>
> - Know that as a parent you will be unpopular at times.
> - Make sure authority figures in the family are operating as a united front.
> - Don't allow yourself to deal in generalities. Be specific in everything that is discussed.
> - Always keep in mind that all consequences need not be negative. Good behavior needs to be rewarded, as does bad behavior that is not repeated.
> - Work double time on maintaining a positive tone and attitude.

But in another way, I wasn't much better. I was authoritarian, and my usual response to the kids was, "Because I said so. That's why!" You can imagine the fireworks when Herb and I tried to decide on Heather's boundaries.

Heather took advantage of our differences and became a master at playing "Divide and Conquer." She knew if she could get Herb and me to argue, she'd wind up doing whatever she wanted. After several fights in front of Heather, though, Herb and I got wise. We started discussing our parental bottom line privately, away from Heather's earshot. Many times we conducted a parent-to-parent arbitration before meeting with Heather. For both Herb and me, this involved substantial compromises, but the effort paid off. We practiced a more balanced, constructive parenting style that worked well with Heather.

It's also important to be specific about everything discussed at arbitration. This includes not only problems, solutions, rules and consequences, but also comments about positive and negative behaviors. Being specific eliminates misunderstandings and helps kids understand exactly what you want them to do. There's a world of difference between these two comments: (1) "You're doing much better with your temper." (2) "I noticed how you handled yourself yesterday afternoon when your brother made you angry at the pool. You made a good choice when you dove into the water to cool off rather than hit him or call him a name."

Before an arbitration, think carefully about important issues. Decide in advance what needs to be said and how you're going to say it. If you have difficulty staying on track during discussions with your kids, list your concerns before the meeting and work through them at arbitration. Also, enter into the process with an upbeat attitude, keeping in mind that, just as in real life, not all consequences are negative. And as I said before, good behavior needs to be rewarded, as well as bad behavior that hasn't been repeated.

One couple started the first family arbitration on a positive note when Dad surprised the group with banana splits. A single mom began with what she called "the positives." She asked every family member to say something positive about themself and every other family member. What a wonderful way to begin!

WHEN DO YOU GET STARTED?

Children who grow up with the workbook and arbitrations consider it a way of life. Our younger daughter, Renee, started on the program at age eight. For several years, she thought every child had a workbook and every family had a Saturday morning arbitration. Starting at a young age allowed our family to have the needed structure in place to navigate easily through Renee's teen years.

For Younger Children

Having children grow up with weekly arbitrations is a terrific preventive measure for future problems. Therefore, seven or eight is an ideal age for most kids to begin participating. For younger children, however, arbitration often serves a different purpose than for their older brothers and sisters. It is utilized mostly as an opportunity to enhance self-esteem and comment on good behavior. For example, one family used this time to again comment on and thus reinforce their youngster's good classroom behavior.

Because younger children have short attention spans, you can't wait until arbitration to correct inappropriate behavior. You need to address misbehavior as it occurs. In their book *Assertive Discipline for Parents*, Lee and Marlene Canter suggest an excellent on-the-spot disciplinary technique called "The Broken Record." With this approach, parents break the discipline into four parts: (1) a request to change behavior; (2) a repeated request to change behavior; (3) the offer of a choice; (4) the follow-through on the choice. It sounds like this:

- "Please stop running in the house."
- "Please stop running in the house."
- "Either stop running in the house or go outside until dinner."
- "Go outside until dinner."[1]

Another effective disciplinary measure is called "Do What I Want First." The principle: A child must complete what the parent wants done before doing what she wants. For example, "Pick up your toys and then you can go outside and play." Or "Take your bath and then you may watch television."

When establishing rules with younger children, many psychologists suggest this great format:

MAKING RULES FOR YOUNG CHILDREN

- Look at the child, ideally on an eye-to-eye level.
- Appropriately touch the child on the arm or shoulder.
- Explain the necessity for the rule.
- Establish the rule and attach a consequence.
- Ask him or her to repeat the rule and consequence to you.
- Write down the rule and consequence.

As an example, when Renee was eight, she kept forgetting to put her bike in the garage at night. Finally one evening, with plenty of focused attention, we told her, "You're having a difficult time remembering to bring your bike in the garage. Instead, you're leaving it in the street, in the driveway, or at the neighbors. Because of this, the rule and its consequence will be: "If you do not put your bike in the garage by 6:00 p.m., you won't be able to ride it the next day." Then we asked her to repeat the rule and consequence and write them in her workbook. After losing her bike on several occasions, Renee was finally able to remember where her bike belonged at night!

Finally, because of their short attention spans, younger children need brief arbitration sessions, usually between ten and fifteen minutes. If you're conducting a family arbitration, attend to the younger kids first, then let them go play while you talk to their older brothers and sisters.

For Teenagers
Utilize the first arbitration to carefully describe the *Parenting Without Pressure* workbook. Before the first meeting, explain that you plan to give

them more control over what they can and cannot do, and that you'll look for tangible measures—following rules, being accountable for fun times and evenings out, completing daily stuff—to assess their behavior. Also tell them what behaviors, determined by your list of dislikes, you would like to see improved or changed. Ask them to think about these behaviors and about fair rules and consequences (if necessary) for these actions.

Some teenagers may resent arbitration and at first be defensive. This is especially true if boundaries and rules have been loosely defined in the past. Inform them gently but firmly that this is a win/win program that is here to stay. Also, occasionally a youngster may dislike the term *arbitration*. Be careful not to get caught up in semantics. Basically, arbitration is a family meeting. Therefore, use a term that works best for your family.

No matter what their age, let your kids know that showing up for arbitration is not an option, but participating in the arbitration is their choice. However, if they decide not to talk at arbitration, parents can unilaterally decide on the operating boundaries, rules, and consequences. Once your kids learn the workbook is here to stay, and arbitration is a chance to be heard and have their needs addressed, they will settle down and learn how to make the program work for them.

After familiarizing the kids with the workbook and giving them (especially the older ones) the oppportunity to think of specific areas they would like to discuss, you are ready to start regular arbitration meetings. Before you get down to problem solving, though, take care of a few important preliminaries.

Point to the positives. Like the single mom I mentioned earlier, start by asking everyone to say something positive about every other family member, including themself. They can praise general qualities or specific actions in the last week, and parents should especially compliment good behavior. Don't worry about verbal overkill. Kids cannot hear enough positives!

TAKING CARE OF FAMILY BUSINESS

With everyone together in a family arbitration, you can make announcements and coordinate individual schedules. At our house, we used this time to fill out the master calendar so everyone would know about the upcoming week's activities and transportation arrangements. After arbitration, we posted this calendar on the refrigerator door. You can discuss anything from dentist appointments to the next family outing. Getting involved in the family's plans helps kids feel like they belong and motivates them to take responsibility and to constructively participate.

Taking care of business at arbitration can also avoid mishaps and misunderstandings. For example, Renee would frequently schedule appointments for the same time I was working. Consequently, this often resulted in a last-minute panic about transportation. We eliminated this problem at arbitration by discussing and listing activities and appointments a week in advance.

Take time to talk. Ask the kids if they have specific items to discuss, leaving your tough arbitration points until later in the meeting. (Once you start arbitrating difficult issues with children, it's hard to move on to anything else.) Letting children talk first allows them to freely discuss anything from the ridiculous to the sublime.

Heather once used this opportunity to exclaim, "Mom, you're making me crazy! You're always nagging me." I listened and took notes as she listed specific incidents that constituted nagging. As I examined my behavior over the next few weeks, I admitted that Heather was right: I said many things of a nagging nature.

After the initial shock, I committed myself to correcting as many of the "nags" on the list as possible, with interesting results. The more I worked on this "nag factor," the more arbitration and I gained credibility with Heather. She realized that I'd meet her more than halfway, and she opened up to changing herself.

Other kids will use this time just to talk. I frequently worked in the evenings, so many nights I wasn't available for Renee. However, she knew she had my attention for as long as she wanted on Saturday mornings. I made myself a captive audience, hanging on to every word. Consequently, Renee's arbitrations meant hearing about her crush on Tom Cruise, her difficulty with her algebra teacher, and the details of her latest argument with her girlfriend.

Because these things were important to Renee, Herb and I made them important to us. We invested a great deal of time and patience, but it was worth it. In the security of arbitration meetings, we deepened the communication with our daughter. Also, on more than one occasion, Renee shifted gears to address more weighty topics that needed attention.

USING THE WORKSHEET

After these preliminaries, it's time to tackle the arbitration worksheet, shown on page 68. It provides a step-by-step guide to discussing specific problems and negotiating rules and consequences.

ARBITRATION WORKSHEET

1. Define the problem. _Renee wants to attend the Valentine's Day dance at school._

2. Let the kids talk. _Present list of phone numbers of people from school for us to call this week. (We will resume this next arbitration.)_

3. Let the parents talk. _We are not comfortable with dance but agree to call people on list._

4. Brainstorm possible solutions. _1. She can go to dance 2. She can't go to dance. 3. She can go & we will chaperone._

5. Choose the best solution. _She can go and we will chaperone._

6. How did it go? _We were able to find a solution we could both live with! Great problem solving by Renee!_

Define the Problem

Before you bring up a problem, ask yourself these questions: Is there really a problem? Is this an issue on which I want to take a stand? Will I need to develop a rule for this? One Mom decided that her sixteen-year-old daughter dressing in black and sporting purple hair was not the problem, so she let appearance go without comment. The real problems were the daughter's drug use and sexual activity.

If the answers to the questions above are yes, then be specific in describing problems to your children. Focus on current behavior only, avoiding the temptation of harping on past actions or projecting into the future. For example, avoid saying, "Oh my gosh! You're failing the ninth grade! You almost failed the eight grade, and I bet you don't do any better next year!!"

Can We Stop Here?

As often as possible, give your kids the chance to correct their behavior without establishing rules or consequences. Since writing out a rule for every behavior can discourage you and your children, try to stop at the request stage. That is, simply ask your children to change and give them the chance to do it.

At age fourteen, Renee had what I thought to be a liberal bedtime: 11 p.m. Over the months she started pushing the limit and getting into bed closer to 11:30. At arbitration, Herb and I discussed the need for her to rest, so we asked that she correct the problem. No rule, no consequence. She respected our request and got to bed on time that week. We congratulated her at the next arbitration and didn't write a rule or a consequence.

With Heather, it took years before we stopped at the request stage. With her will of iron, we couldn't affect her behavior unless we attached rules and consequences to our requests. But by plodding along faithfully and allowing the workbook to work for us, we got to that point with her as well. Believe me, when we finally did, it was wonderful!

Get the Kids' Input
After you've laid out the problem from your perspective, let the children respond, taking as much time as needed. Don't interrupt, react, or place a value on anything they say, especially if your response is negative. As much as possible, show empathy and that you're trying to understand how they feel. If children feel you've listened to and understood them, they're more likely to listen to and understand you.

Reply with Your Input
Because you already stated the problem, you can keep this brief. Simply say, "Here's how I feel about it," and address your child's concerns as well as your own. Take responsibility for your emotions by using "I" messages instead of blaming the kids for your worry or distress. Simply stated, the format sounds like this: "When . . . , I feel . . . , because. . . ."

- Describe the behavior you find bothersome. Simply describe; don't blame.
- State your feelings about the possible consequences of the behavior.
- State the consequences.[2]

Here's an example: "When you run away, I feel terrified because it can be so dangerous being on the street." If parents don't accuse their kids of causing emotional stress for them, the children are much less likely to be defensive and consequently to tune parents out. When you take responsibility for your feelings, your kids are more likely to temper their emotions, let down their defenses, and listen.

In addition to the words you use, check your nonverbal communication. Do you cross your arms? Point your finger at the kids? Sit stiffly in your chair? These negative nonverbal signals can betray your words by revealing anger and resentment. On the other hand, giving plenty of eye contact, nodding when it's appropriate, and leaning forward in your seat can communicate that you care.

Consider All Possible Solutions
After everyone expresses their opinion, explore the possible solutions for the problem. List everything, even the solutions that sound silly. This is a brainstorming session, so everyone should be heard without feeling put down. Then with all of the options on the table, discuss each one by discussing your personal responses rather than passing judgment on the person who suggested it. You can say, "I like that idea" or "I'd have a difficult time doing that."

Choose the Best Solution

With the list narrowed down, work at compromising and creating a win/win situation for you and your kids. Remember to carefully pick those issues on which you take hard stands. This will free you to say no to the important things. One teen was allowed to wear her purple combat boots, but her dad said no to skipping school.

Once a new rule and consequence are established, write them down in specific terms in the workbook and read it aloud for everyone to hear. Be sure that everyone clearly understands because this rule is now in effect. Also be sure to note those areas of agreement or compromise. For example, when we agreed to allow Renee to attend the dance, we wrote it in her workbook. Later, when we had to say no to something else, we easily could refer to this area of agreement and remind her of our willingness to compromise.

Parents, after arbitration take a minute to evaluate your progress. This will guarantee that arbitration is beneficial to everyone and is not being used as a gripe session.

In the end, arbitration is a basic problem-solving skill that is a learned rather than an innate process. It's the basis for good decision making because it teaches children to reason and think. Most important, arbitration can be applied to other areas of their lives. Heather worked throughout her college years, and if she had a problem that warranted a meeting with her boss, I felt sorry for him. I knew she was ready for him. I wasn't sure he was ready for her. By that time,

> **QUESTIONS TO ANSWER AFTER ARBITRATION**
>
> - Was every family member given the opportunity to be heard and their needs addressed?
> - When dealing with problem areas, were you specific?
> - Did you keep on track and stay positive while dealing with tough issues?
> - Did you avoid using arbitration as an emotional release or dumping ground?
> - Did you follow through on the decisions?

she'd become a master at problem solving and arbitration.

KEEPING GOOD COMMUNICATION GOING

Arbitration depends on good communication, but don't reserve open communication just for your weekly table talks.

Communicate in Everyday Life

Good communication flows from mutual respect, understanding, and trust among family members. When children are treated with the same courtesy and understanding that their parents give their best friends, it sends a strong message of love and support: "You are worthy of my interest and time and although we might not always agree, I'll always value your individuality and your right to feel the way you do."

Tough to do? You bet. But how many times have you listened to a heartbroken friend recount a story told many times before? And instead of showing weariness and boredom, you listened with empathy. Do your children deserve any less? Kids need to be heard.

Allow Children to Speak Their Mind

You can accomplish this by valuing what they say, even though you don't agree with it. With Heather, I had to learn the difference between "valuing" and "agreeing." We disagreed on many issues, and it was a relief to realize agreement wasn't necessary. Our lack of agreement didn't automatically make one of us right and the other wrong; it just meant we held different viewpoints. Knowing this, it became easier to value Heather's thoughts and eliminated my need to win her over to my side.

The change in my attitude produced an unexpected side effect, too. When we did deal with issues that were clearly "right" or "wrong," Heather was more likely to understand my point of view when she didn't need to defend hers. Kids need to be valued.

Share Yourself with the Children

Let your kids see you and your spouse as real people. Spend unstructured time together. Attend ball games. Share chores and hobbies. Talk about all kinds of things, not just issues and problems. Really care. You can't miss when you combine listening with respect, trust, and understanding. And by all means, have a great time.

One dad shared with his son his love of remote-control model airplanes. And to his delight, his son expressed an interest in flying them too! Together they spent many enjoyable hours refurbishing and flying old planes. As a result, they had the opportunity to connect on a different level and see each other in a new light.

Choose Your Words Carefully

When asked, most parents will say they want good communication with their children. And yet without realizing it, they're the greatest roadblock. Probably the biggest reason is our pressure-cooker existence today. We live with excessive stress in a fast-paced world, and the homefront can turn into a dumping ground. The pressure, irritability, and exhaustion take their toll. Sadly, children end up on the receiving end of chronic irritability, abusive criticism, insensitive comments, and emotional unavailability.

Compounding this problem is the children's immaturity. Parents can lose sight of the fact that a fifteen-year-old, 186-pound boy is as close to age ten as he is to age twenty—and will act like a twelve-year-old about half of the time. Teenagers are especially notorious for responding to parental dialogue by acting bored, flip, silly, coy, or hearing-impaired. It can cause parents to react with verbal blasts that emotionally cripple kids. Emotional walls are built with the bricks of thoughtless words. And trusting relationships, so longed for, never materialize.

Comments that Build Walls Instead of Bridges

Playing the martyr
- "Are you trying to drive your mom and me crazy?"
- "Why are you doing this to me?"

Placing the blame
- "You're responsible for your dad leaving us!"

- "I spend so much time worrying about you, I can't hold down a job."

Name calling
- "You're pathetic . . . really worthless."
- "You kids today are such weirdos."

Threats
- "Touch it again and you die."
- "I'll send you back to your mom!"

Sarcasm
- "That was real bright, dummy!"
- "I knew I could count on you to screw up."

Comparison
- "Why can't you be more like your brother?"
- "When I was your age, I was a football star."

Criticism
- "You'll never get anything right!"
- "You're a bum like your father."

Contrary to popular belief, kids listen to what their parents say—and they live up or down to parental expectations. If you tell children that they're bad, worthless, or failures, they'll act accordingly. If you tell them they're important, worthwhile, and capable, they'll believe that, too. For that reason, stop and think before speaking to your kids. Say what's uplifting and encouraging so they'll share their lives with you. It's hard for children to trust someone who verbally assaults their self-esteem.

One parent was surprised to learn that his son felt he couldn't talk to him about being tormented by the school bully. Instead, the teen took a gun to school. But then the dad sadly realized he had "shut down" communication long ago by referring to his son as stupid, a cry baby, and a wimp. Naturally, the father was the last person the youngster felt he could trust.

Arbitration helps families build the foundation for positive family life. By providing parents with a practical format, they can eliminate daily fighting and clearly communicate expectations. Children learn the important skills of problem solving and good decision making. And everyone learns to recognize, value,

and treat one another with dignity and respect.

MORE TIPS ON KIDS AND COMMUNICATION

1. Always treat children with courtesy, respect, and kindness.
2. Talk with your kids, not at them or down to them.
3. A child has a right to her feelings. Mutual respect involves accepting those feelings.
4. While children are speaking, don't mentally rehearse your reply.
5. Listen more, talk less.
6. Don't interrupt when your children are speaking.
7. Listen actively by repeating back your child's feelings with empathy and understanding.
8. Be available.
9. Make sure your nonverbal communication is positive.
10. Cool off before you talk. Remember, if you want to be listened to, you first must listen.

HOMEWORK FOR PARENTS

1. Identify any negative statements or comments you would like to eliminate from your vocabulary today and then do it!

2. Discuss the arbitration concept with your children. Carefully explain how this family meeting time can work for them and what it can do for the family.

3. Have your first family arbitration.
   a. Start with the positives.
   b. Comment on good behavior.
   c. Take care of family business.
   d. Deal with specific issues.
   e. Stay on track and follow through.
   f. Be positive! Be positive! Be positive!
   g. Assess how you did.

4. Commit yourself to not discussing the contents of the workbook or anything confrontational or argumentative except at arbitration. Work on improving the emotional atmosphere of the home daily.

CHAPTER SIX

Tots and Teens

Is there really much difference?

If you have experienced life with a two-year-old and now have the privilege of living with a teenager, you'll have to agree that there doesn't seem to be much difference! Both can be extremely negative and rebellious as they experience turbulent changes in their quest for identity and independence. By understanding the dynamics of the many physical and emotional changes occurring with adolescents, however, parents can often help calm the stormy seas of their fantastic rite of passage into adulthood.

To better understand teenagers, many parents draw from their own experiences as young people. For the most part this can be a mistake, because their memories tend to be distorted. Some recall the teen years as being packed full of the carefree experiences of "Happy Days." For others, it was more like "West Side Story," with a ten-block walk to school through sleet and snow. Whatever the case, however, parents tend to remember those "Wonder Years" as either perfect or having been handled perfectly well.

The problem, of course, is that parents often can't grasp the reality of how it is for their youngsters because their focus is still on how it

was for them. It can be frustrating for a teen to be continually measured by Mom and Dad's experiences, which often produce unrealistic standards.

COPING IN THE CORRIDORS

It is easy for a teenager today to be overwhelmed and frightened by the reality of his world. Tragically, some youngsters must contend with things at home such as divorce, poverty, abuse, and neglect.

At school they don't fare much better. Not only must they struggle to pass English, math, and science, but many must also cope with drugs, violence, and sex among their peers. Unfortunately many of these same youngsters are confronted with either being ignored or ridiculed and taunted by their classmates.

Because insecurity runs rampant on school campuses, kids can be very vicious. To make themselves feel bigger and better, they verbally attack anyone they perceive as different. A child can easily find his dignity stripped and his self-esteem badly damaged.

School is a child's workplace. However, his choices are very limited and legally he can't quit until he is sixteen. One hundred eighty days of the year, school is a place he must go and contend with whatever he finds.

Fortunately, for most children school is a positive experience that equips them with the tools to lead full, productive lives as adults. However, for too many others, school is disastrous. In the corridors and classrooms these kids are often forced to negotiate emotional mine fields without adequate coping or problem-solving skills. When coupled with immaturity and lack of experience, trouble is almost sure to follow.

Many times parents fail to realize that it's important for children to feel good about themselves. Too often parents trivialize some of their children's painful experiences. The exercise that follows might help you understand more clearly how some kids end up feeling after a school day.

Imagine

Imagine it is tomorrow morning and you are getting ready for work. As you stand in front of a full-length mirror, you carefully examine your reflection. You start by studying your hairstyle. You scrutinize your face, inspecting your eyes, ears, nose, and mouth. You examine your body frame, your weight, and look at the size of your hands and feet.

As you continue to stare at the mirror's reflection, you begin to think about your job and the particular tasks you perform. Now imagine that when you get to work you are ignored. Even though you were out sick for several days, no one realized you weren't there. People walk around you, look at you, and maybe even speak to you if it's necessary, but they really don't see you. You are never sought out for advice, and never included in office gossip. No one asks you to go to lunch. You find that you are a nonentity. How do you feel?

There is one thing worse than being ignored, however.

Imagine that you find your particular job very difficult. Even though you honestly try, you are often ridiculed because sometimes you do your job poorly. When you make a mistake, it is quickly pointed out by someone who implies to your coworkers that you are a real slow thinker or maybe even just plain stupid. Someone might even suggest you are slightly retarded. In fact, they make "Retard" your new nickname. The office staff loves this because your inadequacies provide them with more than a good time for those long afternoons.

Also imagine that even though

you carefully dressed for work, the office fashion critic is all too quick to point out to the others that your clothing doesn't match, doesn't fit, isn't in, or isn't very expensive. In fact, what you have on could be considered a real Goodwill special. You are deemed a real nerd. When the crowd doesn't call you Retard, they call you Goodwill Special.

Now think about your hair and imagine that someone asks, "Did you do that to yourself or did a lawn mower run over your head?" You're also likely to hear, "And you actually wear glasses? It's obvious you don't realize that glasses make your nose look soooooo big and your ears stick out! Also, you really need braces. And by the way, is that a pimple or a mole?"

Finally, imagine that the comments turn to addresses, and yours is discussed at great length. Everyone knows that living in that area of town must mean you are poor, which means that you are less than important. If your address doesn't reveal your all-too-important financial status, your car will. Some

coworkers can't believe you actually have the nerve to be seen in something so archaic. What a relic! But then, that's what they expect coming from a family like yours. The conversation ends when someone asks, "Why did you even bother to come to work today? This place would be better off without you."

Does this exercise exaggerate the point? Somewhat, but if you listen carefully to many young people today, you'll realize that this illustration is not far off. Unfortunately, when comments such as these are heard often enough, they gain credibility in the mind of a young person. When teenagers are asked today to describe the popular kids in their schools, they talk in terms of money, looks, and brains. If a child happens to be missing one or all three and he doesn't happen to be a star athlete . . . watch out!

CHANGING IN THE HALLS

While kids are trying to cope with these ridiculous standards of measurement for their self-worth, they are also undergoing tremendous physiological and emotional changes. The wonderful time in life known as puberty is responsible for these drastic changes.

Because of better diets and health, puberty is occurring at an increasingly earlier age. The average age for menstruation for girls in the United States is 12½. During this time, energy levels of a teen will dramatically fluctuate because of the continual hormonal changes. A youngster can be full of energy one day, only to suffer from extreme fatigue the next.

Due to a teen's increased metabolic rate, he will experience an increased appetite and rapid growth. Watching a teenager eat a meal during these times of rapid growth can be a startling experience for parents, second only to trying to keep groceries in the house.

The physical growth experienced by a teen during this time will be unparalleled except by the first two years of life. For example, it is not unusual for a youngster to grow five inches and gain twelve pounds within a year. Just when he becomes somewhat comfortable with the way he looks, he is suddenly faced with another spurt in growth that adds inches and pounds. Different parts of the body grow at different rates because this explosion of growth doesn't follow a consistent pattern. Consequently, the youngster who could move effortlessly through the corridors at school one day suddenly finds himself tumbling over his hands and feet the next. And the clothes that fit last month become tight as the bathroom scale records another pound or two.

Teens spend endless hours examining their reflections as they search for any flaw or imperfection that wasn't there yesterday. The questions they most frequently ask are, "Am I getting fat?" "Does this really look all right?" "Am I too tall?"

One of the cruelest jokes Mother Nature can play occurs during the early teen years, when kids are their most insecure. To compensate for their insecurity, young teens long to be carbon copies of one another. Yet the biological clocks of adolescents are not synchronized. This can cause havoc for a young girl who develops

CHANGES TO EXPECT IN TEENAGERS

1. Extreme mood swings
2. A struggle for independence
3. A search for their identity
4. Peer group importance
5. Self-centeredness and instant gratification
6. Heightened sexual awareness
7. Fragile self-esteem

much earlier than the other girls and finds herself heads taller than everyone in the class except the teacher! Or still worse is the ninth-grade young man who still looks like a twelve-year-old and sounds even younger.

Knowing what to expect eliminates the element of surprise when these physiological changes take place. And it enables parents to prepare children for the many accompanying emotional changes as well.

Extreme Mood Swings

Because of a teen's tremendous hormonal changes, his emotional state is unpredictable, to say the least. David Veerman summed it up nicely when he said, "A teen's behavior is like the weather in Chicago. If you don't like it, wait around a minute and it will change."[1] Parents can easily become bewildered, confused, and exhausted as their youngster rapidly goes through his entire range of emotions. Although these highs and lows are expected, they can exasperate parents.

Often these extreme mood swings are referred to as a teen's roller coaster of emotions. This term best described what Heather often experienced. She would be happy and laughing and then miserable and crying within seconds. Unfortunately, it was some time before we learned to stay off Heather's roller coaster. On more than one occasion, my entire family's temperament was determined by fourteen-year-old Heather's emotional state.

Heather's displacement. During this time Heather displaced much of her anger and unhappiness. She was often miserable and was convinced we were responsible. Many times I found myself caught up in her moods and would take personal responsibility for them. I spent fruitless hours trying to appease her. Years later I finally learned not to take responsibility for Heather's emotional state. And by detaching myself from it, I no longer took her conduct or comments personally. Instead I concentrated on being a constant in Heather's continually changing emotional state, the anchor she could hold on to.

A Struggle for Independence

A child needs to move away emotionally from her family before she can ever move away physically. Unfortunately, this can be an eye-opening experience for Mom and Dad. Until the teen years, the family has been the dominant group from which the child has drawn her identity, and most parents bust their buttons at this. Boy, do parents love it when a child mirrors their thoughts, feelings, values and attitudes. "She is just like her mother" can cause any mom to burst with pride.

Imagine the surprise parents feel when, around age twelve or so, a daughter no longer wants to be Dad's little girl and has struck out on her own—or at least has gone as far as the nearest peer group. During the teen years, it is this group that a youngster usually looks to as she struggles to put some distance between herself and her family.

Putting this distance between the child and her family is usually accomplished in several ways. One of the most common is for the child to make a statement with her clothing, usually by dressing very differently from Mom and Dad. The results are interesting, with kids wearing everything from micro-minis to combat boots!

Seeking out parental flaws and very self-righteously giving the parent a detailed report is another way a youngster puts some distance between herself and her family. Heather was great at this. For example, she would continually compare me to all her girlfriend's mothers: "I can't believe you are about the same age as Sally's mother. She is so much younger looking! You really should have her teach you how to dress. Her clothes are so hot!" "Get with it Mom. Your hairstyle went out ages ago." "You're not going to wear those shoes again are you? They look so dumb!" On and on she would go.

A parent's best bet at this point is not to be resentful, to exercise patience, and to be the very best support mechanism possible as the child moves away. This can be accomplished only if the parent remembers not to take the child's conduct or comments personally!

Many teens experience ambivalent feelings about being independent young adults. Often they struggle with the conflicting feelings of wanting to be a little child again and desiring total independence, all within minutes. These mixed desires can be very bewildering for youngsters and can leave parents totally confused. Again, be patient with your children's struggle as they try to figure out who they are apart from the family.

A Search for Their Identity

This is a time when youngsters try to discover who they are, and to formulate thoughts, feelings, and attitudes that are uniquely their own. Developing an identity separate from the family is a slow process that at times can be challenging.

This stage of life is much like a child going into a stranger's closet and trying on all the clothes. He isn't sure what he likes until he can see how it looks and feels on him. And just because he happens to have something on one day, that doesn't mean he'll wear it for a lifetime. Thus, kids will have purple hair one week and a buzz haircut the next.

This process was best depicted by the adolescents of the '60s. The parents of this group of young people were a very conservative lot. Dad, having just fought in World War II, did two things his father probably never did. With financing from the Veteran's Administration, he bought his own home. And with the GI bill paying his way, he went to college. The adjective most frequently used when describing a good husband and father of this era was simply "good provider." Dad worked long and hard, and both parents placed a high value on materialism and an education.

You can imagine the excitement that was generated, therefore, when their children hit the adolescent years and began questioning and experimenting with the values and goals of their parents. Yes, this was the group that put flowers in their hair and hitchhiked to San Francisco. Mom and Dad went ballistic. What happened to those kids and where are they today? Take a look around. Many of them are probably your neighbors and friends who have MBAs, stock portfolios, and expensive cars.

During this time of change, the very worse thing a parent can do is panic and start to use labels. Continually saying to your teen, "You are just a punk!" might be the very thing that convinces her that she is. Be sensitive and tell your children you love them not because of what they are wearing but because of who they are.

Peer Group Importance

During this time, peer groups take on considerable importance. When a teen first starts to move away from the security of the family, he is still far too fragile and vulnerable to stand alone. So he will look to his peer group for the guidance and support he needs. By watching his friends, a teen learns how to dress, dance, talk, and—unfortunately at times—even how to act. This is a time for testing values, attitudes, and feelings, and for experimenting with all of these and more.

This peer group will offer a sense of belonging and provide ways to be admired and accepted. It also will become a learning laboratory. By watching his peers, a teen can develop new social skills such as compromising, negotiating, and interacting. And finally, from this peer group will probably come his first opportunity to date.

Having a child be influenced by a negative peer group is every parent's nightmare. Often in an attempt to protect kids from danger, parents resort to desperate measures that usually include grounding the child for life and telling him his friends are rotten people. Both are sure to backfire. Yet what is a parent to do?

It is important for parents to remember that children want to be listened to, taken seriously, and loved unconditionally. They also have an incredible need to feel they belong and that they count.

A parent's first line of defense is to make sure your child is getting all of these things at *home*! Work hard on building a relationship with your child. Listen without being judgmental and ask him for advice or for his thoughts on a particular subject. More important, even if you do not like his behavior, make sure you communicate your unconditional love and acceptance of him.

Additionally, remind your child that he is capable of making good choices, and when he is in doubt about participating in some group behavior to simply ask himself these questions: Is this illegal? Is this immoral? Is this something I should not do at this age? Could it hurt me or anybody else? Could it make a difference in my life in five years? If he can say no to those questions, he probably will be OK. Also remind him that if he is still in doubt about doing something, he can always ask you or someone else he can trust. And let him know that you can always be used as an excuse: "I want to, but my parents would ground me forever."

Finally, remember that not all peer groups are bad. There are many good groups of kids in schools, churches, and the community. Parents should do whatever is necessary to expose their children to positive influences, even though it will take a commitment of time by the parents.

Self-Centeredness and Instant Gratification

Teenagers can be extremely self-centered and demand immediate gratification. They can easily become consumed with themselves. Much of this is because of the rapid changes they are undergoing, especially during early adolescence. They never quite get a chance to grow comfortable with the way they look before they've changed again. Therefore, *me*, *myself*, and *I* are favorite pronouns.

Adolescents become obsessed with what they are going to wear, how they are going to fix their hair, what they are going to say to this person or that person, and so on. And because they are so obsessed with themselves, they are usually convinced everyone else is as well. This is why a pimple on her chin can send a kid into orbit, and why a thirteen-year-old can spend two hours getting ready to help her mom with the grocery shopping.

For many teens, this is a time of immediate gratification and instant results. Unfortunately, this doesn't necessarily get better as they get older. Because they see it happen on television all the time, they believe every problem can be solved in thirty minutes with two commercials, or one hour with four commercials if it is a really big problem.

Working is a great experience for many teens. It can enhance their self-esteem and teach responsibility. However, it also can add to the problem of teens experiencing instant gratification. Because much, if not all, of the money a teen makes can be used for her discretionary spending, rarely does she choose deferred gratification. It is no longer a question of saving for a new blouse or pair of shoes. If she wants something, she simply gets it immediately.

Dr. James Gardner, author of *Understanding, Helping, Surviving the Turbulent Teens*, suggests, "The teenager's frequent need for immediate gratification seems to be a left-over childhood tendency simply not yet outgrown."[2] The ability to postpone gratification is one of the major marks of maturity. Parents should start early in developing this area of their children's maturity.

Heightened Sexual Awareness

Although statistics tell us that more teenagers are becoming sexually active earlier, most of them are incredibly ignorant about their own bodies and sexual feelings. And because much of what they learn concerning sex comes from television, music, movies, and friends, teens often tragically confuse the concepts of sexuality, love, and intimacy. Our young people certainly deserve better.

Parents need to equip teenagers with the knowledge that will enable them to make sound choices and take responsibility for their own sex-

uality. Unfortunately, many parents are reluctant to do so for fear that this information will cause their children to become sexually active. And yet studies have proven that just the opposite is true.

Additionally, it is vital for parents to continually share their values, attitudes, and beliefs with their teens and to encourage them to make decisions about being sexually active before, not after, the fact. Parents also should inform their youngsters that not everyone is having sex. Most of the kids who say they are . . . aren't! Encourage your children to wait. Being a teenager is tough enough without the added dimension of being sexually active.

Dr. Kevin Leman, author of *Smart Kids, Stupid Choices*, states, "Sex is a wonderful gift, and when used and developed correctly, it can be very beautiful. But it is not a way to build a solid, lasting relationship. The very act of sex, which can bring new life and joy, can also, through misuse, bring destruction and devastation to many lives."[3]

However, Heather said it best when as a college student she wrote to her younger sister:

Why wait? Having sexual feelings is normal, and having them doesn't make you a bad person. However, when you act on those feelings as a young person, it is easy to lose your balance. Believe me—this is not the time for acting on them.

Adolescence is a time to learn how to be friends, to trust your feelings, to take care of yourself, to be responsible, to set goals, and to discover who you are. Because things are out of sequence when you add a sexual dimension to your life as a teenager, it's easy to lose learning all these things in the sex.

Also, it is tough enough sorting out your thoughts and feelings for someone when you are not sleeping with him. But once you start sleeping with him, it can prove to be an impossible task. This is because everything becomes very exaggerated.

Decide before, not after, the fact about being sexually active. And then build in whatever safeguards you think are necessary to keep that commitment to yourself. Be good to yourself and wait. Love, Heather

For teenagers, abstinence is the only way to go. However, if a teen is already sexually active, telling him not to be is not going to make him stop. Only a healthy self-esteem and a decision made by him will do that. But what is at stake is far too important not to make sure he has the information to act responsibly. That might be very hard for some parents to do, but today the risk of an unwanted pregnancy or contracting a sexually transmitted disease (including deadly AIDS) has to be considered.

The following list serves as a tool to create open lines of communication about sex, as well as a reminder to parents to carefully hear what their teenagers are saying.

Be informed. Kids today are extremely misinformed. But guess what? So are many parents. Make sure your information is correct. When parents provide erroneous information, they often lose credibility with their teens. Don't hesitate to check out your local bookstore or library if you need some education in the area of sexual behavior.

"I HEAR" CHECKLIST FOR PARENTS

1. Be informed.
2. Be honest.
3. Be early.
4. Be available and askable.
5. Be realistic.

Be honest. Kids need to know where their parents stand. Share your values and beliefs with your youngsters. Also, don't be afraid to tell your teens that while having sex is a very adult behavior, it does not make adults out of teenagers! Being sexually active without the emotional maturity that only years and experience develop can be and often is a nightmare for many young people.

Be early. Start early with your children. Waiting until they are adolescents to discuss sex is too late. Instead, continually answer your children's questions and provide information in an age-appropriate way as they are growing up.

Be available and askable. Create an open, ongoing dialogue about sex with your children regardless of their gender. Use news items, television programs, and the radio as opportunities for discussion. Help your children feel comfortable about asking you anything! Be careful not to be judgmental in your comments or to nonverbally say, "Don't ask me that!"

Be realistic. Think about the world kids live in today and the sexual messages they are bombarded with constantly. In a year's time, a youngster is exposed to 15,000 references to sexual intercourse, with less than 150 of them mentioning birth control or abstinence.[4] Given these numbers, it's not surprising that in 1990 approximately one million teenagers became pregnant.[5] Faced with this reality, today's parents are learning that telling teens "No!" does not keep them from having sex. Teach your teens how to make informed choices.

Fragile Self-Esteem

Many young people suffer with fragile self-esteem. Self-esteem is simply how you feel about yourself. Few teenagers like the way they look, or feel acceptable to the opposite sex. In fact, Dr. James Dobson tells us that 80 percent of teenagers do not like the way they look.[6] Unfortunately, the worse kids feel about themselves, the more willing they will be to conform and to buy a sense of worth by doing what everyone else in the group is doing.

More than anything else, a healthy self-esteem will enable teenagers to say no to alcohol, drugs, sex, and misguided peer pressure. They will be able to take care of themselves by making good choices and sound decisions.

BEING PREPARED FOR CHANGES

Change can be frightening, especially if it catches a person unaware. This is especially true of teenagers as they first experience the many changes of puberty. A little preparation—by carefully explaining to children the many things to expect—can go a long way in preparing everyone for this transition.

In addition to explaining the changes, you might want to make a list of the thoughts and feelings a teenager will probably experience during this time. Then put a date on the list, tuck it away in a safe place, and wait. When the going gets tough—and it surely will—get out the list, note the date, and read it.

Many times during her teen years, we pulled out Heather's yellowed list and lovingly reminded her of what we had talked about years before. And more important, we assured her that she wasn't always going to feel the way she listed on paper.

Gently remind your child that the problem is not with you or with him or her. It is this particular time that every teenager has to go through.

FEELINGS TEENAGERS MAY EXPERIENCE

1. Nobody likes me . . . especially Mom and Dad.
2. I feel ugly.
3. Nobody understands or cares.
4. Any place would be better than here.
5. I feel like running away from home.
6. I just wish everyone would leave me alone!
7. My parents treat me like such a baby.
8. I feel like crying all the time.
9. Sometimes I feel like I am going crazy.

BEING PREPARED
FOR WHAT'S NORMAL

Let's face it. A great deal of a teenager's behavior gives parents the opportunity to develop important character traits such as patience, understanding, and a very high tolerance for frustration. Fortunately, most of what kids do is benign. However, it helps for parents to remember that although fifteen-year-old Junior is 6 foot 4, he still is a little guy! Dr. Ross Campbell says it best:

> 1. Teenagers are children.
> 2. Teenagers will tend to act like teenagers.
> 3. Much of teenage behavior is unpleasant![7]

How true! All parents of teenagers have shared similar experiences that validate this. For example, young teenage boys love to cup their hand tightly under their armpit and squeeze down forcefully with their arm, thus making a very strange noise. And teenage girls insist on carrying all their makeup, hair spray, brushes, combs, mouthwash, perfume, nail polish, every note ever written, and pictures of every friend they have had in the past five years. Somehow, all of this fits in their purses, which they periodically leave at school, in restaurants, and the car.

How many of you know of a kid who has worn bowling shoes home from the bowling ally or left all his school books on the bus? Also, with older teens, what is the very first thing you do after you get into the car that your teenager has just driven? Right! You turn down the radio, even before you turn the ignition on!

None of these things is fatal—just annoying. But knowing what to expect, and having realistic expectations of teen behavior, can go a long way toward a peaceful existence.

COPING WITH THE FOUR B'S

Many young people suffer from feelings of inferiority. If you ask any boy or girl in junior high or senior high school to describe the most popular kids at school, *beauty*, *brains*, *bucks*, and *brawn* are the words you'll hear. This can be pretty frightening for parents who believe their children are lacking one or more.

David Veerman, in his article titled "Skin Deep—Preoccupation with Physical Appearance," lists these excellent suggestions parents can use to help their youngsters cope with the distorted sense of values that many teens use to measure worth.

"Don't Be Surprised"
It's normal to want to be accepted, to dress up for one's peers or a special person. In this regard let's not judge hastily. We adults do the same thing. We follow fashion gurus religiously. Analyze your wardrobe and think about how often you check your own appearance.

"Don't Condemn"
Parents should gently help their teenagers understand the necessity for cultivating deeper, more important qualities such as love, compassion, honesty, loyalty, integrity, and self-discipline. And parents should affirm those qualities in their children and their friends.

"Understand the Problem

Our standards are all infected by society's sickness. Studies show that beautiful people tend to be favored in school, politics, and business. Our kids live with this reality—from class officers to homecoming royalty. They need to know adults struggle as well."[8]

The problem has been around for a very long time, and to some extent we have participated in it. Take a good look at the children's stories that your kids (and possibly you) grew up with. What was wrong with Dumbo, the flying elephant? His big ears! Sleeping beauty was envied because of what? Her beauty. What happened to the ugly duckling? He turned into a swan!

Also, take a look at the toys we buy our children. Oregon State University researcher Elaine Pedersen and her colleague Nancy Markee examined Barbie and fifteen other fashion dolls. The results were very interesting. The researchers found that if Barbie were life-size, her measurements would be 31-17-28. Waist measurements on the other fashion dolls would range from 17 to 23 inches and they would be 6.2 to 7.5 feet tall. No wonder many young girls have a problem with their body image!

"Feel Their Hurt

It's easy to dismiss your child's situation as a stage or growing pains, but the pain is real."[9] Help where you can.

Unfortunately, in the area of appearance, I wasn't the least bit compassionate with Heather. I felt that conformity was a ridiculous measurement of a person's worth,

COPING WITH THE FOUR B'S
■ Don't be surprised.
■ Don't condemn.
■ Understand the problem.
■ Feel their hurt.
■ Steer them into areas of affirmation.
■ Remind them of your love and acceptance.
■ Purge personal prejudices.

and I wasn't going to buy into it. During this time, young girls had to have Jordache jeans. I felt that no child of mine was going to advertise a manufacturer by wearing a product that had a label or name stamped on the seat of the pants. I was firm in my stand, and for a long time Heather did not have her Jordache jeans. Instead, she opted for safety pins in her ears and a very strange color on her hair.

What exactly did I accomplish in my stand? Nothing positive. At a time when it was crucial for her to conform, I said no to a desire that was very safe.

Now does this mean that as parents we have to refinance the house to keep our kids in designer clothes? Heavens, no. But offer them alternatives. For example, many parents offer a clothing allowance or a specific amount for a special article of clothing or shoes. If the child wants an expensive item such as $100.00 sneakers, simply provide the money you would have spent on the shoes and help him find ways to make up the difference.

Parents also should be sensitive to other areas where they can help. For example, basic hygiene. Did you know it is quite possible for a fourteen-year-old boy to shower with a bar of soap in one hand and a washcloth in the other and never get his back wet? A parent might need to help in this area.

Basic grooming might need to be addressed. Something as simple as a new hair cut, contact lens, braces, or a trip to the dermatologist can make a world of difference. Help where you can!

"Steer Them into Areas of Affirmation

Many sports don't emphasize size. Soccer, swimming, cross-country running, tennis, and gymnastics actually favor smaller competitors and have gained national prominence and popularity. There's more to life than football. Parents can find creative alternatives. Most high schools provide a smorgasbord of extracurricular activities, many of which provide excellent training for the future."[10]

Children will always gravitate toward those things that make them feel good about themselves. Therefore, it is very important that we provide positive activities for them.

A child who seemingly has no outside interests can be a challenge. However, a parent can help simply by identifying the uniqueness of that child. Help him or her recognize special interests, skills, and strengths. These can become a talent or a hobby that provides a refuge in the storm for an adolescent. Teach him or her to compensate for weaknesses and never to compare those areas with someone else's strengths. Affirm your child whenever possible and always praise effort.

ACTIVITIES KIDS MIGHT CHOOSE	
Bowling	Dance
Gymnastics	Swimming
Band	Drama clubs
School paper	Girl Scouts
Boy Scouts	Little League
Soccer	Tennis
Jobs after school	Chorus
Big Brother and Big	Piano
Sister programs	Skating
Youth groups	Boys Club
Service clubs	YMCA programs

"Remind Them of Your Love and Acceptance

It is not too cool for teens to admit that they enjoy their parents' affirmation and affection, but we must not stop offering it. Teens long for acceptance from their parents. Your words and actions will often make the difference in their lives."[11]

Tell children often that they are loved and are important to you!

Purge Personal Prejudices

"As parents, we must be sensitive to our own lives. Our actions and careless words can quickly betray prejudices and contradict all that we have tried to teach our children."[12]

ADDITIONAL SELF-ESTEEM BUILDERS

Fritz Ridenour, in his book *What Teenagers Wish Their Parents Knew About Kids*, suggests these excellent ideas for building self-esteem. One by one, we slowly incorporated these things into our everyday lives with Heather.

Ridenour's first suggestion is, "Decide on some specific things you will concentrate on this month and

the coming months to build your teenager's self-esteem."[13] By narrowing our focus, we identified one important aspect of Heather's self-esteem we felt needed immediate attention and started to work on it.

We concentrated our efforts on helping Heather feel more competent. When a child feels competent, she takes a can-do attitude. Feelings of competence, however, are based and built on successes. With Heather we looked for anything that could be considered a success. Many times these were mini-successes or even partial successes, but for our purposes they still counted. And once counted, we then would offer praise, appreciation, and encouragement. An excellent tool to use when doing this is home economist Barbara Gregg's list of "100 Ways for Parents to Show Appreciation."[14]

Another of Fritz Ridenour's suggestions that we used was, "Be generous with the compliments, but be sure you are sincere and on target. Teens can smell a phony compliment every time. Sometimes on the surface they aren't too receptive to well-deserved praise, but keep com-

100 WAYS FOR PARENTS TO SHOW APPRECIATION

1. You're on the right track now!
2. You are very good at that.
3. That is the best you have ever done.
4. I am happy to see you working like that.
5. Nice try!
6. That's the way to do it.
7. I knew you could do it.
8. Now you've figured it out.
9. Now you have it.
10. Outstanding.
11. Keep working at it. You're getting better.
12. You're working hard today.
13. You're a great help!
14. You're getting better every day.
15. You're really growing up!
16. You figured that out fast.
17. You're a real prince (or princess).
18. You did that very well.
19. Nice going!
20. That was a kind thing you did.
21. Keep it up!
22. Super!
23. You make it look easy.
24. When I'm with you, I feel like singing.
25. I sure am happy you are my child.
26. That's my boy (or girl)!
27. I'm very proud of you.
28. I'm proud of the way you worked today.
29. You can do it!
30. You'll do better next time!
31. I think you've got it now.
32. Keep trying!

100 WAYS FOR PARENTS TO SHOW APPRECIATION (continued)

33. You've got it down pat!
34. Good thinking!
35. You've just about got it.
36. You are doing that much better today.
37. You are really going to town!
38. You're really improving.
39. I love you!
40. Superb!
41. That's much better!
42. That's really nice.
43. I like that.
44. Fantastic!
45. That's right.
46. You must have been practicing!
47. I appreciate your help.
48. One more time and you'll have it.
49. Sensational!
50. Nobody's perfect.
51. You certainly did well today.
52. You're doing beautifully.
53. Congratulations!
54. That is quite an improvement.
55. That's a masterpiece.
56. Excellent!
57. That's the best ever.
58. You're doing fine.
59. You are learning fast.
60. That's it!
61. Couldn't have done better myself.
62. You really make being a parent fun.
63. Terrific!
64. You did it that time!
65. You haven't missed a thing.
66. Now you've figured it out.
67. That's the way!
68. Dynamite!
69. Keep up the hard work.
70. Nothing can stop you now!
71. Good for you!
72. You've got your brain in gear today.
73. Wonderful!
74. You did a lot of work today!
75. Nice going.
76. Now that's what I call a fine job!
77. It's a pleasure to be a mommy (or daddy) when you work like that.
78. You've just about mastered that!
79. Right on!
80. Good remembering!
81. You are really learning a lot.
82. You've got a great future!
83. Fine!
84. You're doing the best.
85. Tremendous!
86. You outdid yourself today!
87. Perfect!
88. You remembered.
89. Now you have the hang of it.
90. Great!
91. Well, look at you go!
92. That gives me a happy feeling.
93. That's a friendly thing to do!
94. Clever!
95. You're like a beautiful (name object), (child's name).
96. Way to go.
97. Marvelous!
98. You're beautiful.
99. Congratulations! You got (name the behavior) right.
100. Lovely!

ing at them. Underneath they appreciate it."[15]

Remember, many times this involves taking the time to identify areas where parents can compliment a child. Kids do neat things all the time, but because parents become accustomed to those things, they no longer compliment their children. For example, when a child has kitchen duty and has done the job well, there is a tendency for many parents to say nothing. Unfortunately, the child will hear a comment only if the job has been done poorly.

Parents, focus on everyday things, perhaps now taken for granted, and be generous with your compliments.

And finally, we took this Ridenour suggestion to heart: "Be patient with their impatience, their tendency to label you as old-fashioned, out-of-date, ancient. It's amazing how modern you will become in a few years if you last."[16]

Heather was always quite annoyed that I was so old-fashioned. All the other girls were doing the very things she was not allowed to do, or so she thought. Often she would scream, "You are single-handedly trying to destroy my social life!" and "Lighten up and get with the times!" However, I hung in there. Interestingly, as Heather grew older, she became very protective of her little sister. Often I heard Heather say, "Mom, you are not going to let her do that, are you?"

Our patience through the years with Heather's impatience really paid off.

HOMEWORK FOR PARENTS

1. Discuss with your youngster the physical and emotional changes that occur during adolescence. Talk about some of the emotions he or she might experience during this time. Then list them and tuck the list away for future reference.

2. Review the "I Hear" Checklist for parents. Create open lines of communication with your teens concerning their sexuality.

3. Identify specific areas where you can help your youngster enhance his or her self-esteem.

4. Incorporate "100 Ways for Parents to Show Appreciation" into your everyday vocabulary with your children.

CHAPTER SEVEN

Saved by the Bell

Making school a positive experience.

School is a training ground for children, with the primary goal of preparing them for life as adults. Unfortunately, kids can perceive school as an "end" rather than a "means to an end." They fail to understand that classwork teaches them to reason, analyze, and conceptualize. And these skills help them, as adults, to find ways to effectively handle problems at their jobs, with their families, and in their relationships.

Several years ago, the ABC special "American Kids: Teaching Them to Think" noted that by the year 2000 the average factory job will require at least thirteen years of education. Instead of strong backs, employers will look for sharp minds as the demand for workers with computing, reasoning, and problem-solving skills continually increases. The uneducated adults of tomorrow will be unable to compete in the workplace and will be ill-equipped to handle the complexities of the twenty-first century.

What does this mean for your children? It's important that they make the most of their time in school, and that you help them learn and prepare for the future.

THE VALUE OF LEARNING

Because parents serve as a window to the world for their children, your values and attitudes easily rub off on your kids. This is especially true with younger children. If, for example, you think poorly of a teacher or believe that education is a waste of time, your kids probably will, too. In 1983 the National Commission on Excellence in Education published a report entitled "A Nation at

Risk: The Imperative for Education Reform." Parents were told, "As surely as you are your child's first and influential teacher, your child's ideas about education and its significance begin with you."[1]

In light of this statement, it's vital for you to maintain a positive attitude when talking to your children about school, and to continually stress the importance of an education. Starting in preschool, you can encourage children to value learning. As they grow older, you can reinforce the idea that dropping out of school isn't an option for them.

Help children establish clear goals and see an education as a way to achieve those goals. Also help them see that an education can enable them to realize a productive, exciting future of untold possibilities.

How Parents Can Help

Parents first help children in school by taking an interest in their education. At home, take the time to instill basic values and provide plenty of love and discipline. Set appropriate guidelines not only concerning behavior in the classroom but for assignments as well.

Read daily to younger children and help them develop a love for books. Provide positive reading material by subscribing to fun, educational magazines and a daily newspaper. Also acquaint youngsters with the public library and establish a family library day once a week or once a month.

Be a positive role model. Enroll in a class at a local college or through an adult education program at a high school. Read and study together. Make learning a family affair!

Establish a structured study time and a quiet place to complete homework. Keep a good dictionary and plenty of school supplies on hand.

Never take anything for granted and continually check your child's school progress. Just because a parent has not heard from the school does not automatically mean all is well with the child. Information should be obtained from both the school and the child at arbitration. Also, determine the number of academic credits needed in each subject required for graduation and continually be aware of your high school student's status.

Start a school file for each child and find a safe place for it. Develop the habit of carefully reading everything you receive from school. In each child's file keep all relevant school correspondence as well as standardized test results and report cards. This is an excellent place to keep deadlines and requirements for scholarships, loan applications, and admission applications for college-bound students.

Attend school orientations and meet teachers, noting their names, the subjects they teach, and the class periods they teach your children. Also get information about the best time to contact them concerning school-related matters. Again, all this information should be kept in the children's school files for quick reference.

Tell the teachers and school administrators that you are interested in your children's academic progress and request that you be told immediately of any problems.

Strong evidence suggests that

HOW PARENTS CAN HELP

- Take an interest in your child's education. Attend school orientations and other school-related activities.
- Instill basic values that provide plenty of love and discipline.
- Read daily to younger children and provide plenty of positive reading material for older kids.
- Be a positive role model. Make learning a family affair.
- Establish a structured study time.
- Start a school file for each child. Develop the habit of carefully reading everything from school, and keep important information in your child's file.
- Celebrate a child's accomplishments big and small.

the more parents become involved in their children's education, the better those children will do in school. Teachers are much more likely to take an interest in a child when they know the parents. Parents can make sure a child doesn't become just a name on a roster by getting involved. Develop good parent-school and parent-teacher relationships. Consider becoming a room mother or father or a chaperone for school field trips.

Finally, parents, attend school-related activities such as athletic events and awards programs. Celebrate a child's accomplishments big and small. Whether he is the star quarterback or spends most of the time on the bench; whether she wins the spelling bee or makes it through only half of the cuts; celebrate your child's success and reinforce his or her participation.

PROBLEMS AT SCHOOL

When youngsters do have problems in school, they usually can be categorized into four major areas.

Discipline

If a child cannot exercise self-control, he is going to have a difficult time in the classroom. Usually (but not always) a child who has a discipline problem in school has received little or no consistent discipline at home. It is vital, therefore, for parents to understand the importance of instilling discipline, values, and standards for conduct early in a child's life. Failing in this will only handicap the child as he struggles with self-control and appropriate conduct in the classroom.

In some cases, however, the child might not be able to control his behavior. Children who are emotionally handicapped, that is, afflicted with hyperactivity, attention deficit disorder (ADD), or attention deficit disorder with hyperactivity (ADHD) can experience severe behavioral problems.

Misbehavior in the classroom might also be the result of alcohol or drug abuse on the part of the teenager. The number-one drug problem among teenagers today is alcohol abuse, and a great deal of drinking is done on junior and high school campuses.

Possible Solutions

A. Understand that the responsibility of instilling discipline, values, and standards is the parents' and not the school's. Start early in teaching children self-control and appropriate classroom behavior.

B. Set boundaries that include behavior in school. This might mean weekly progress reports or even daily behavior progress reports for younger children. Be sure to reward the behavior you want repeated!

C. Consider enrolling your child in an athletic program that stresses discipline and self-control.

D. If the behavioral problem has been ongoing, request that the child be tested to determine if there is an emotional handicap, hyperactivity, or another disorder. If a problem is diagnosed, immediately address the needs of that particular child with the school psychologist. Medication and therapy might be necessary.

E. If the youngster has an alcohol or drug abuse problem, seek immediate treatment. Getting stoned or wasted should never be tolerated—anywhere!

F. Anytime a child is chronically angry, full of rage, and acting out, consider individual or family therapy. The inappropriate behavior might be a symptom of a much bigger underlying problem.

Academics

Because kids rarely want to admit that they have trouble learning in general or a particular subject, acting out becomes a safe alternative. It is very important to young people that others don't perceive them as slow or not very bright.

In fact, a youngster who is failing school might be very bright but hampered by something else. She might not know how to study effectively for a test, or might lack the discipline to complete homework assignments.

Also, many times a child can suffer hearing or vision loss or even dyslexia and not be aware of it. The child who seemingly won't learn perhaps is one who simply can't learn.

Finally, a youngster might not be interested in school. Or he might simply be bored with the classes he is taking and is underchallenged.

Possible Solutions

A. If a child is chronically failing, request that he be tested to determine if there is a learning disability. Ask the school psychologist to help assess the test results and aid in determining the best course of action. If there is a learning disability, consider private tutoring with a

learning problem specialist. Also consider an alternative educational program that specializes in small classes and individual attention.

B. Make sure the child is in good physical health. An exam with your family doctor might be necessary. Have his vision and hearing checked. If glasses are needed, make sure he likes the frames and is comfortable with the way they make him look. Most teenagers would rather not see and fail than wear glasses they don't like.

C. Assess the child's diet. Teen years are a time for very rapid growth that requires better nutrition than hamburgers and potato chips. Also, because of rapid growth, a teen may have difficulty functioning on six or seven hours sleep at night. Make sure she gets plenty of rest.

D. If the child is bored, determine why. Seek help in directing him toward more intellectually challenging classes.

However, if he is bored because he is just not interested in school, consider alternative education programs. For example, during a youngster's junior and senior year, many schools offer programs that allow students to go to school half the day and work the other half.

College isn't for everybody. The military service provides excellent opportunities for high school graduates. Good careers can be found by working in a trade.

Social Acceptance
Often social problems can be more troublesome to correct than academic problems. A child who suffers from poor self-esteem often will suffer socially at school. "Low self-esteem is the single most powerful root cause of America's steadily increasing public school dropout rate," states Professor Hayman Kite.[2] According to Tammy Austin, coordinator of a short-term truancy intervention program, "Especially at risk are second-semester sixth grade students. The transition between elementary and middle-school is very difficult for some children and they get lost in the peer-pecking order."

Kids that don't fit in socially will often go to any lengths to do so. Unfortunately, because of their incessant need to belong, many adolescents will become involved with any peer group that takes them. They also might turn to alcohol or drug abuse or sex as they struggle for peer attention and acceptance. Or they might simply withdraw, develop a negative outlook about school, or a defensive attitude toward those around them.

Also, truancy becomes an option for some teens who feel frightened and intimidated because they are being physically threatened.

Relationship problems with a boyfriend or girlfriend can cause a youngster to take a nose dive at school. Because these relationships tend to be intense, they can become all-consuming. Fortunately, most are short-lived.

Finally, a youngster could be influenced by a peer group that has already dropped out of school. Algebra can be tough to tackle if you know your best friend is tackling the beach or even a job to pay for his new Camaro.

Possible Solutions

A. Understand the importance of a youngster's feelings and her need to belong. Parents should do whatever is necessary to help a youngster feel better about herself. This might include helping with her clothing or grooming. Also, basic social skills are not necessarily innate qualities: A crash course on making friends or how to be a friend might be very beneficial. Additionally, some specific behaviors might alienate her from other children. For example, is she loud or obnoxious?

B. Provide opportunities for positive peer group interaction apart from school such as special hobby clubs, organized sports, or church youth group activities. Contact the school guidance counselor if your child is being teased or ridiculed. Peer counseling or a mentor program might be made available. If a child is being threatened, make an appointment with the school guidance counselor and principal and insist that the problem be addressed. Put this request in writing and ask that it be included in your child's file at school.

C. Take your child's romantic relationships seriously, be available, listen and care.

D. In as subtle a way as possible, limit the amount of time your youngster spends with friends who have dropped out of school.

Home Environment

Every family has its own set of problems. Unfortunately, the more serious of these problems might include such things as relationships between family members, unemployment,

---

ADDRESSING BIGGER SCHOOL TROUBLES

- Make sure information cards at school contain the correct information about your child.
- With the school psychologist review a child's cumulative file at school to determine if testing for learning disabilities is needed.
- If truancy is a problem, request a personal phone call rather than a recorded message notifying you of the absence.
- Before suspension occurs, request in-school suspension.
- Request weekly progress reports.

---

divorce, poverty, and alcohol or drug addiction of family members. Serious family problems do not always have to be detrimental. However, these types of difficulties become destructive if children see their parents collapsing under the weight of their problems.

Possible Solutions

A. Watching parents constructively deal with major problems can actually benefit children. It provides them with the opportunity to learn important concepts such as problem solving, decision making, stress management, and goal setting. Often we could tell Heather when she was having a problem, there isn't a problem in having a problem. The problem is in not doing something about it. "Every problem has a solution. We just have to find it!"

B. At times, finding the best solution to the problem might involve tapping resources outside the family, such as professional counseling. By doing this, you teach children one place to go for help.

ADDRESSING BIGGER SCHOOL TROUBLES

1. If the child's behavioral problem has been ongoing, ask to review his school file. Parents now legally have a right to see their children's records. Ask the school psychologist or guidance counselor to review the records with you. This will enable you to better understand the various test scores, teacher assessments, and behavioral labels such as ADD or ADHD.

2. At the beginning of each school year, make sure *you* fill out all information cards requested by your child's school. This will eliminate the possibility that his records contain incorrect information or false signatures. Some kids will list their personal phone numbers as the number to call to report school absences and sign their parents' names. Then they can receive important phone calls from school and sign their parents' names on progress reports, etc.

3. A parent can have his child's school records flagged so that if she is absent from school, a counselor from the guidance department will notify the parent instead of the parent being notified by a recorded message.

If truancy is a problem, determine why the child is skipping school and address that problem area. Establish a rule concerning skipping school with an appropriate consequence.

For example: "You may not skip school. To do so will result in either Mom or Dad going to school with you the very next school day." The parent can take a folding chair, a thermos of coffee, and a very good book and escort his younster from class to class. (Always check with the school administration prior to doing this.)

4. Before a suspension occurs, request that the child be given only in-school suspensions. Instead of a three-day holiday at home, the youngster then will be required to spend three days at school on suspension.

5. Request weekly progress reports for all the child's classes. At arbitration establish a rule that includes a required weekly grade point average in each class and a consequence for not having it.

CONFERENCES

When a problem arises at school that requires a teacher conference, first

---

QUESTIONS ABOUT PROBLEMS AT SCHOOL

1. What is the problem as you see it?
2. How long has the problem been going on?
3. How well do you get along with this teacher? Do you have the same problems with other teachers?
4. Do you understand the subject material?
5. Do you participate in class?
6. How would you describe your behavior in class?
7. How well do you get along with the kids in this class?
8. What kind of solution do you see to the problem?

address the problem at length with the child at arbitration. Carefully explain the problem as it has been presented to you and ask the child the following questions. Take detailed notes about his answers. If the youngster won't respond, list these questions and ask him to answer them in writing.

Once you have a clear understanding of the problem from the child's perspective, make an appointment for a parent-child-teacher conference. A positive parental attitude when dealing with the school administration or individual teachers is important. When addressing specific problems, be cooperative rather than defensive, and don't try to place blame. Implement a win-win approach with a statement such as "How can I help you help my child in this area?" Ideally, this will enable everyone to work together to help the child.

At the parent-child-teacher conference ask the teacher basically the same questions you asked the child. Again take detailed notes. Compare answers, examine the facts, and identify a specific problem or problem areas. Then brainstorm all solutions to the problem. Again, make sure your attitude is non-threatening and is one of helping the teacher help the child.

If you strike out completely with a teacher and are totally dissatisfied, there are additional steps that can be taken. However, make sure the problem is serious enough to warrant going further.

1. Consult with the principal. Using your conference notes, present the facts to the principal and ask him or her to mediate. Again, be sure to take notes of the meeting.

2. Go to the school board. Again using notes you took at the teacher's conference and your meeting with the principal, present the facts to the school board and ask them to mediate.

3. Look for alternative educational programs. They may be the only solution when a youngster is having extreme difficulty, is at risk of dropping out, or has already dropped out of school.

4. Finally, remember that all teachers and guidance counselors are not the same. As in all careers, some people are better than others. A good math teacher can mean all the difference in the world for a youngster struggling with the basics. And a good guidance counselor can help teens and parents assess test scores and detect and correct problem areas. Always be on the lookout for teachers or guidance counselors that can best help your youngsters. Before school starts, request those people.

HOMEWORK FOR PARENTS

1. At the beginning of each school year, request from the school a calendar of important dates. Add to your master calendar all relevant school dates such as orientations, open houses, and holidays.

2. Establish a school file for each child in the family. Develop a habit of reading all the materials from school and filing important information.

3. Take an active interest in your child's education. Attend school activities and functions. Celebrate accomplishments both big and small!

4. Express excitement and interest in the different subjects your child is learning. Emphasize the importance of your child's education and its application to the real world.

CHAPTER EIGHT

How Can I Love You?

I'm not sure I even like you.

Loving a child when you are not sure you like him or her is very much like a high-wire act. It calls for some extraordinary balancing and excellent concentration, and it can prove to be exceedingly difficult. Loving a child you may not like calls for basic unconditional love. Above all else, unconditional love provides the cornerstone for the emotional well-being of a child.

Surprisingly, you start with loving yourself unconditionally. To have an impact on children today, especially those who are troubled, parents need to be at their very best.

Perhaps I can clarify this best with the analogy of the lifeguard and the swimming pool. Imagine sending your child, who is a poor swimmer, to a pool with all his friends for an afternoon of fun and frolic. Being a good parent, you would call to ask about the lifeguard. How frustrating it would be if your conversation went something like this:

"My son doesn't swim very well and wants to spend the afternoon at the pool with his friends. Please tell me about the lifeguard who will be on duty."

"Certainly! This particular lifeguard is very well liked by all the kids who swim here."

"Wonderful!" you might reply, "But how well does he swim?"

"Well, he is really dedicated to saving youngsters. In addition to that, he is an excellent student and involved in many extracurricular activities. He really is the type of kid who would make any mother proud."

Again, you might reply, "Great! But can he swim?"

"No, as a matter of fact, he can't swim. But he sure is a real nice guy!"

Would you still let your youngster go? Probably not. Instead you would ask, "How in the world can this lifeguard be expected to save anyone if he cannot even save himself?" His intentions may be very honorable, but to be effective at his job, he has to be strong and capable in the water.

Families are like that. Good intentions are great, but to deal with children effectively, parents need to be strong and capable. Fear, worry, and resentment are difficult to govern and anger almost impossible to control if a parent is physically and mentally exhausted. Like the lifeguard, a parent can help others only when he can save himself.

Start by taking responsibility for taking care of yourself. Putting a premium on yourself by treating yourself with dignity has an interesting effect: It forces others to do so as well.

Too often parents put "doormat" signs on their foreheads and let their rights, needs, and desires be trampled upon. Too often they allow their own identities to become tightly wrapped up with their children's. They feel that only by sacrificing their own lives can they win their children's good behavior, sympathy, and love. Sadly, the only thing accomplished is that the parents become martyrs and are neither appreciated or respected by anyone, especially their children.

This is exactly what took place in my home. Heather had two standards of conduct: one for our home and one for everywhere else. I discovered this only after continually hearing from neighbors and friends how wonderful and well- behaved Heather was. My Heather? The one with the four-letter-word vocabulary and howitzer mouth?

Then I realized that of course she was wonderful—there! Heather knew that if she pulled the stuff next door that she was pulling at home, she would promptly be shown the door with instructions never to return. Other folks liked themselves far too much to put up with any verbal bashing from my teenager.

What lesson did I learn? Only when you treat yourself well will others treat you accordingly. Then and there I took "doormat" off my forehead and learned how to take better care of myself.

Dr. Merrill F. Raber and Dr. George Dyck list ten steps for maintaining mental fitness in their workbook *Mental Fitness: A Guide to Emotional Health.* These ten steps provide an excellent guide for those who want to enhance their self-esteem.

For years I had a difficult time dealing with stress, anger, and resentment. I kept things bottled up until I exploded and acted in totally inappropriate ways. Because stress is cumulative, it soon took very little to trigger my temper. And at times I acted like a complete fool. Then, of course, I felt guilty about what I had done, which only added to my stress, and so it went. For example, once when Heather and I were grocery shopping, we had a terrible argument and caused quite a scene. To this day I cannot remember exactly what we fought about. However, what happened during the argument is very clear. The memory of that day

TEN STEPS FOR MAINTAINING MENTAL FITNESS

1. **Become Aware of Your Own Needs.** The first step is to accept yourself. Remember, the unconscious part of your brain really knows you. When you force yourself to act differently, it will show. If your life is unduly boring—or if you feel put upon or neglected—admit it and do something about it, rather than saying, "This is the pits."

2. **Let Your Needs Be Known.** Clearly express feelings without attacking others. This will avoid allowing negative feelings to build up and be expressed either internally as stress or externally as inappropriate behavior.

3. **Demonstrate Behavior That Reflects High Self-Esteem.** This can be accomplished via body language and attitude. If you look alert and interested and follow with a smile, others will recognize the good feelings you have about yourself.

4. **Work to Improve Yourself By:**
   - Learning—Read, enroll in academic or self-improvement classes, or work with others.
   - Challenges—Do something new every few months that seems interesting or is fun.
   - Health and Appearance—Improve your nutrition and get adequate rest and regular exercise.
   - Spirit—Spend time with optimistic people, follow a spiritual program, and work on projecting a positive attitude.

5. **Stop Negative Value Judgments About Yourself and Others.** Become aware of how much energy goes into judging others versus finding unique strengths in others to admire and relate to.

6. **Allow and Plan for Successes.** Emphasize what you do well. Build on your strengths and value that part of you. Remember that all successful people have regular failures but do not allow themselves to be defeated by them.

7. **Think Positively.** Think about your good qualities. Give yourself credit. Keep a "What I Like About Myself" journal.

8. **Learn to Escape When Appropriate.** It is good to meet problems head-on, but sidestepping may be desirable at times. People set unrealistically high standards and become frustrated when they are not achieved. Learn to add variety to your life by planning interesting (not especially expensive) activities. Don't wait for someone else to make your life interesting.

9. **Find Ways to Help Others.** Refocus your attention on the needs of others. Identify ways you can give to others (for example, volunteering for a community project, getting involved in a church program, finding someone who needs companionship). Above all, show interest in others during normal conversations.

10. **Be Willing to Seek Help When Required.** When you have problems, find people with whom you can share them. If problems seem overwhelming, it is appropriate to seek professional help, particularly if the intensity of the feelings does not diminish after sharing them, or if feelings of worthlessness or low self-esteem persist.[1]

is imprinted on my brain forever.

Heather had become an expert at punching my buttons. She did so that day with her usual flair. Only this time I didn't think through the problem so I could respond with a cool head. Instead, I reacted very badly. In the bakery section, I bashed, belted, clobbered, and walloped Heather with a loaf of Wonder Bread. As my anger subsided, bread crumbs lay on the floor and bread dust fell from the air. With tears in my eyes and bread in my hair, I stood in horror and gasped at the substantial crowd that had gathered. Heather stood there covered with bread, looking innocent and sweet. She smiled and said, "Well, I guess I should be glad we were not in the canned goods aisle."

Yes, I was a real candidate for some remedial work on taking better care of myself.

According to Patricia Jakubowski in her book *The Assertive Option*, parents have some very basic assertive rights:

A PARENT'S BASIC RIGHTS

1. Act in ways that promote your dignity and self-respect as long as others' rights are not violated.
2. Be treated with respect.
3. Say no and not feel guilty.
4. Experience and express your feelings.
5. Take time to slow down and think.
6. Change your mind.
7. Ask for what you want.
8. Do less than you are humanly capable of doing.
9. Ask for information.
10. Make mistakes.
11. Feel good about yourself.[2]

STRESS MANAGEMENT

Because stress was a real problem for me, learning how to cope more effectively with it became a real priority in my life. Dr. Penny Lukin, a psychologist, makes several excellent points on stress management. She states, however, that first it is important to recognize the signs of *distress*, or ineffective coping: giving up and becoming depressed; experiencing an inability to concentrate; becoming argumentative, irritable, anxious; or developing stress-related illnesses such as heart palpitations, insomnia, headaches, high blood pressure, neck and back pain, ulcers, or stomach aches. Walloping Heather with a loaf of bread was a definite sign of ineffective coping!

Also important, Dr. Lukin notes, is to eliminate the threat of stress by putting yourself in control and finding appropriate ways to manage your stress. She suggests the following:

Lower expectations of yourself and others. Becoming more realistic with your expectations is both freeing and empowering. Only when Heather and I were freed from my unrealistic expectations of being the perfect mother of a perfect daughter could we become all that we could be!

Take a stress break. A stress break is any activity that gives you a new perspective and reduces your stress. This can include going to the movies, watching TV, reading a good book or magazine, fishing, sewing, talking to a friend, taking time for a hobby, or on a larger scale, a camping trip or mini-vacation. What will work for one will not work for another. The important thing is to find what works for you!

Work off tension through physical exercise. A good physical workout not only relieves tension but also improves your stamina and produces a sense of confidence and well-being. This might include jogging, swimming, walking, biking, tennis, gardening, or working out.

One of the first things I did in my stress management program was to join a health spa. When I felt the stress build, I worked out instead of allowing it to accumulate and possibly explode. For example, one evening Heather and I had a terrible argument. However, rather than reacting and dumping my frustration and anger on Heather, I went to work out. Terribly distraught, I found myself at the spa, riding a life cycle on level five (which is the most difficult level) as I wept into a towel. I still chuckle whenever I remember hearing one young attendant saying to the other that night, "I know it's time to close, but I am not going to tell her she has to get off the bike!" For years, working out helped me keep my sanity and my stress under control. The bonus, of course, was that I also felt great.

Avoid self-medication such as drugs or alcohol. Alcohol and drugs such as tranquilizers are depressants that will depress you and your system!

Eating a balanced diet is important. Pam Smith, an Orlando nutritionist, states, "A stressed-out person's blood sugar may fluctuate wildly, causing mood swings, irritability, fatigue, and food cravings." Unfortunately, the food we crave the most (usually something chocolate!) during times of stress is not what our body needs. Ms. Smith suggests we include in our diets complex carbohydrates for energy, avoid fats and sugar, eat lightly and more often, drink plenty of water, and cut back on stimulants such as caffeine and nicotine.[3]

HUMOR HELPS

Raising teenagers is serious business, but you may be taking yourself a little too seriously. While taking Heather very seriously, I learned to keep things in perspective and not to take myself all that seriously. Everything didn't really have to be a matter of life or death. Besides, Heather took herself seriously enough for both of us.

Realizing that Heather's conduct was not directed at me helped me. Here was a kid who at times was out of control, but her behavior was not directed at me. Granted, I often caught the fallout, but that was all it was.

Mary G. Durkin, in her book *Making Your Family Work*, suggests that you can lighten your burden— and make the task of parenting more rewarding—if you learn to laugh. Writes Durkin, "When you trip, humor will soften the fall. You can then approach seemingly unsolvable family problems with the old cliché, 'If I don't laugh, I'll cry.'"[4] Psychiatrist Christian Hageseth describes a sense of humor as a broad, optimistic perception of life, and suggests that it can ease tension and improve communication.[5]

By keeping my sense of humor and lightening up a little, I learned that Heather and I could actually have a little fun. It's important to remember, however, never to confuse humor and ridicule. Laugh *with* your children, never *at* them. And teach all the family members that a good time should never be at the expense of one person in the family.

TIME MANAGEMENT

Manage your time and energy wisely. Learn to establish goals and set priorities. Simplify your life as much as possible. Be realistic about what is important and needs to be done today, and then make a list of those things. Believe it or not, there are only twenty-four hours in a day. A sure way to burn out is to cram thirty-six hours of activity into twenty-four.

Instead, realistically allocate time to each item on your list of important things that need to be done. Always make sure you include time for yourself. If you find that you have too many things to do and not enough time, put the unfinished things first on your list of things for tomorrow. Does this mean at times you don't get everything done? Yes, it does. But it also means you will finish the race because you have conserved your energy by pacing yourself. Parents can avoid burning out only by avoiding emotional and physical overload.

Working Moms and Single Parents

For a long time women struggled with the myth that they could have it all and do it all. Weekly, we watched Clare Huxtable as she (without help) managed a successful law practice, maintained a beautiful home, and took wonderful care of the needs of her large family. She was never frazzled, she always looked great, and she never served TV dinners. How in the world did she do it? She didn't. Clare was a fictional character. There really aren't any supermoms.

In the real world, only with careful planning and a great deal of help from family members can working moms and single parents successfully juggle career and family. To do a better job of balancing home and career, consider incorporating the following suggestions into your family routine.

Make a list of everything that

needs to be accomplished at home in order for things to run smoothly. Be sure to include all household tasks such as cleaning, errands, yard work, grocery shopping, laundry, menu planning, meal preparation, and making lunches. Then, as much as possible, relax your standards and delegate these jobs to family members. Use the Daily Stuff section of your children's workbooks to assign these tasks. For example, rather than having a specific day to clean house, assign a housecleaning chore daily.

Make grocery shopping a family affair. For years my family made this a family outing. Our evening would start with an early dinner at a local cafeteria followed by our weekly grocery shopping. Because there were four of us, we usually could complete this task in less than thirty minutes.

Park your grocery cart in a central place and divide your grocery list among family members. Even younger children are capable of getting the cereal and dog food. However, make sure everyone sticks to the list to avoid overspending. The added bonus, of course, is that you have plenty of help putting away the groceries!

A major stressor for many working moms is meal planning. Plan weekly menus, thus eliminating morning decisions concerning dinner. Always double recipes and freeze half. Post an on-going grocery list on the refrigerator and encourage all family members to add items to this list when they see the supply running low.

Food preparation can be made easier by requiring teens or older family members to prepare an evening meal once a week. Younger children can assist by setting the table or making a salad. Assign a teen or older family member the task of making lunches for the next day.

Assign a laundry day for each child and require him to be responsible for his laundry. Younger children who cannot master the washer and dryer are great at folding things like washcloths and towels.

Allow teens to "purchase" car time by running errands such as going to the cleaners or taking the dog to the vet.

Finally, it is important for single parents and working moms to provide decompression time when the family comes home in the evening. Establish a coming-home ritual that includes either taking the telephone off the hook or leaving the answering machine on for the first thirty minutes everyone is home. Provide a healthy snack to take the edge off hunger until dinner is served. Allow yourself twenty minutes of uninterrupted time to relax and unwind by taking a nap, walking around the block, or taking a leisurely bath.

One single mom recently shared the success she was experiencing balancing family and career. She had been on the verge of burnout because it had become easier to do things herself rather than go through the hassle of getting her four kids to help. "For years," she exclaimed, "I felt in control of everything but my home life, which was in total chaos. However, by implementing the Parenting Without Pressure program, I now have a method to restore order and allow us to work as a team!"

Because weekdays were often hectic, she organized the upcoming week for the family on Sunday afternoons. After determining which household tasks needed to be accomplished, she assigned these to the kids by filling out the Daily Stuff section of their workbooks for the entire week. On a daily basis, she made additions and revisions and added personal notes. Everyone knew up front what was expected of them for the following week. And for the first time, Mom could count on the cooperation of her children.

FINDING RESOURCES OUTSIDE THE FAMILY

Find resources in the area that can help make your job as a parent easier. Surround yourself with a circle of friends whose advice and judgment you respect, folks you can count on to listen, to care, to understand. Solicit support from an extended family when you can. Also, religious organizations offer great adult support groups and activities for young people. Organizations such as the Big Brother and Big Sister programs and Boy Scouts and Girl Scouts are excellent for youngsters. Many organizations and clubs will sponsor kids who need financial help to participate in sports programs. Most telephone directories have a Human Services listing of organizations and services for adults and young people. Find what is there for you. Consider it a fact-finding mission! Be creative and innovative.

Summers can be a nightmare for a working mom with school-age children left unattended at home. Because summer programs at the Boys Club and YMCA fill up rapidly, one mom starts calling in January for her children's placement. In June, when many parents are frantically looking for something their kids can do, this mom isn't stressed. Talk about great planning!

SEEKING PROFESSIONAL HELP

Parents need to take control of their lives rather than to allow circumstances to take control of them. By establishing goals, setting priorities, and planning, not only will you know where you want to go, but you will learn how to get there. If you hit an obstacle with a child, or if stress is continuous, never hesitate to get professional help. By talking with a competent counselor, insights are realized and new direction obtained. Many organizations and agencies such as churches, mental health centers, and family services provide excellent counseling.

TAKING CARE OF SIGNIFICANT RELATIONSHIPS

Finally, in addition to being very good to yourself, spend time focusing on and maintaining your marriage or significant relationship. Everything tends to get lost when dealing with children in crisis, especially relationships between the adults in the family. Unfortunately, marriage is a frequent casualty in such cases. Couples tend to concentrate all their available energy on the misbehaving child. That child can easily become the focal point of the family. Conversations, family outings, work schedules, and even needs of the other children in the family become secondary to the dysfunctional child.

What an impossible situation for the family and a terrible burden for the child. You may need professional help in learning how to shift your focus. Behavior patterns become habits, and habits are hard to break. This is one behavior pattern that is very destructive and should be eliminated immediately.

Upon realizing that this was happening in our own family, Herb and I set about changing it. It had been a very long time since we had emotionally connected and talked about anything other than Heather. One of the neatest things my husband and I did during this time was to work on getting reacquainted. We learned to schedule date nights and make them a top priority. During those dates, our children and their problems were forbidden conversation topics. Instead, we worked on recreating or developing similar interests and activities apart from the children. One objective was more important, however. We worked at keeping a sense of fun, intimacy, and romance alive in our relationship.

One of our funniest moments occurred during this time. During dinner on one of our first date nights, I endearingly looked up at my husband and exclaimed, "My gosh, Herb, is that you? When did you lose your hair?"

When couples make maintaining the marriage a priority, the results permeate the entire family. Not only does it make the family unit stronger and more capable of handling adversity, it puts that challenging child where he belongs—in the role of a child in the family.

Once you have accomplished these two things—taking care of yourself and taking care of your marriage or significant relationship—you have established a firm base from which you can show your children that all-important unconditional love.

HOMEWORK FOR PARENTS

1. List those activities that help you unwind and relax. Commit yourself to doing one of these things daily for the next week.

2. List non-related job activities that you are doing. Ask yourself, "Do I really need to be doing this?" If the answer is no, take it off your list.

3. Practice time management. Buy a daily calendar. Make a list (in order of priority) of those things that need to be done daily. Remember to include time for yourself. Practice working your way through the list, remembering that those things not accomplished are simply rolled over to the next day.

4. List those things you enjoy doing as a couple. (This can include going out for an ice cream cone or dinner and a movie.) Establish a weekly afternoon or evening date with your spouse and observe it consistently.

CHAPTER NINE

Loving Unconditionally

*Providing the cornerstone
for emotional well-being*

Conditional love is just that—love that is conditioned on something. A person who loves conditionally says, "I'll love you if you do something to make me proud." That something might be doing well in school or excelling at a sport. Often, conditional love is accompanied with expectations that are almost impossible for a child to meet. How many times have you seen a boy trying to please his father by being the star quarterback, or heard a disheartened girl explain why she made 95 percent on an exam rather than 100 percent, or heard a discouraged teen say, "What's the use? There is no pleasing my parents anyway."

Tragically, this parenting pattern often produces kids who either spend a lifetime trying to please a parent or simply quit trying. And sadly, like most dysfunctional patterns, it tends to repeat itself. The child becomes an angry and bitter adult who was unable to measure up as a young person and now sets unrealistic expectations for those around him.

A person who loves unconditionally says, "I love you no matter what—no matter what you look like, what you act like, what you happen to do, or where you happen to find

yourself in life. My love for you is not based on your love for me or on anything else." I will forever remember the words of Mrs. Bundy on the eve of her son's electrocution for his rape and murder of a Florida schoolgirl. Ted Bundy, convicted mass murderer, heard his mother say, "You'll always be my precious son." Wow, talk about unconditional love!

Because as parents we are but mere mortals, total unconditional love is impossible to obtain. But the closer you can come to it, the healthier your family will be. It takes a mature person to look at a little one with all her imperfections and convey to her that not only is she loved immensely, but she is a person of immeasurable worth. Oh, for years I strived for such maturity with Heather!

LOVING THE LEPER

Putting emotional distance between you and your child's behavior is perhaps the most important thing you can do. More than anything else, this will enable you to consistently give your child unconditional love.

Kids who are emotionally and behaviorally out of control can go right for the jugular when dealing with loved ones. Many of these kids are capable of causing unbelievable emotional pain with their howitzer mouths and four-letter-word vocabularies. Such kids commonly target one parent and become experts at knowing that parent's vulnerabilities. They then unrelentingly attack those areas, causing indescribable pain.

When this happens, hurt and angry parents tend to square off and verbally retaliate. Unfortunately, with this kind of response, some parents begin a destructive, vengeful cycle.

My ability to put some emotional distance between Heather's behavior and myself was instrumental in helping me during those devastating times. I learned to emotionally deal with her as if she had some terrible illness such as leprosy. Uncontrolled leprosy can make a person very unpleasant to be around. He will look, smell, and act dreadfully, and in his discomfort he can cause others agonizing pain. Heather didn't have leprosy, but she was suffering, and she definitely was unpleasant to be around.

If a child with leprosy was causing his parents unbelievable anguish, they wouldn't strike back or abandon him. Instead, they would maintain their focus on him, not his behavior, and do whatever was necessary to make him well. My ability to do this with Heather took practice. Because my heart often was bruised and broken, I worked on responding with my head, knowing that in time my heart would follow. Like riding a bicycle, with time and practice I got better and better at it.

BEHAVIORAL WAYS TO SHOW UNCONDITIONAL LOVE

Walking children through tough times involves learning some basic communication techniques that perhaps have been overlooked. In his excellent book *How to Really Love Your Teenagers*, Dr. Ross Campbell differentiates between verbal and behavioral orientation. Adults, he explains, can effectively communicate verbally because they are verbally oriented. Children, on the other hand, are not. They are more behaviorally oriented. Saying to your child all the things that create warm, fuzzy feelings is great and needs to be done often, but it is not enough. According to Dr. Campbell, the two most effective ways to communicate love to your child are through eye contact and appropriate physical contact.

Yes, we really do communicate with our eyes. Often our eyes act like windows to our emotions and our feelings. Dr. Campbell states, "Without realizing it, you use eye contact to express many feelings—sadness, anger, hate, pity, rage and love. In some homes, there is amazingly little contact between parents and teenagers. What exists usually is negative, as when the teen is being reprimanded or given specific instructions."[1]

How sad to think that we look at our children only when we are telling them to do something, or when we are unhappy about something they have done. Many parents will probably stop here and say, "Wait a minute! I talk to my child and look at her when I do!" But do you really? Much of the conversation that takes place with children happens when parents are doing something else.

Many times Heather and I talked, all right, but I also did something else at the same time. I finished up paperwork in my office, washed dishes, or just straightened up the house. Looking back, I realize how frustrating it must have been for her. It was as if I said, "That's nice, dear, but not really important enough for me to give you my undivided attention."

When I realized the importance of this, I worked on taking the time to stop what I was doing, look her in the eyes, hang on to every word, and communicate. I also made sure my body language said, "I enjoy spending this time with you." And finally, I worked on treating her as I would my very best friend. By doing these things, I validated her worth and importance to me. As Heather's parents, we took this step first in a conscious effort to envelop Heather in our unconditional love. Again, it was not so much what we said but what we did as her parents.

Another great way to show a child unconditional love is through appropriate physical contact. Dr.

Campbell stresses the importance of touching your children physically. "Appropriate and consistent physical contact is a vital way to give your teenager that feeling and conviction that you truly care about him. This is especially true when your teen is noncommunicative, sullen, moody, or resistant. During these times, eye contact may be difficult or impossible. But physical contact can almost always be used effectively."[2] Parents really can touch their youngster's heart by appropriately touching her. This might be a slight back rub, a toss of her hair, or a friendly pat on her shoulder or hand. Although it may seem insignificant, parents are sending a powerful message to their teen. They are communicating, "You are important to me and worthy of my interest and my time."

As Heather had grown older, I had stopped tucking her in bed at night. When I started looking for opportunities to touch her and tell her how much I loved her, I resurrected this bedtime ritual. I waited until she was just dozing off. As I sat on the side of her bed, pulled the covers up snugly around her shoulders, and stroked her hair, I told her how very special she was and how much she was loved by her father and me. And then I always added, "Heather, please don't give up on us . . . because sweetheart, we are never giving up on you."

THREE INTEGRAL PARTS TO A PERSON'S SELF-ESTEEM

Dr. Maurice Wagner, in his book *The Sensation of Being Somebody*, talks of three integral parts to a person's self-esteem: feeling you belong, feeling you are worthwhile, and feeling you are capable. Parents should incorporate these into their everyday lives with their children. According to Dr. Wagner, "Feeling you belong starts and stops at home. It is that feeling you get when you know that you are loved, cared for, wanted, enjoyed and you belong."[3]

THREE INTEGRAL PARTS TO A PERSON'S SELF-ESTEEM

1. Feeling you belong.
2. Feeling you are worthwhile.
3. Feeling you are capable.

Making an out-of-control child feel he belongs can be very difficult (especially when half the time you can't stand the sight of him), yet it is crucial to his emotional well-being. Parental anger and frustration often are perceived as rejection by these challenging kids. Unfortunately, many times this results in alienating them even more from the family. Kids who become involved in gang activity are desperately looking for a place to belong and be accepted. University of Houston sociologists recently conducted a study on teen gangs that confirmed this. They found the primary reasons for joining gangs were to feel accepted and needed.[4]

As much as possible, we want to pull these kids back into the family and let them know that they are cared for, enjoyed, loved and accepted at home. Again, this can be difficult, but it can be made easier by separating the child from his behavior.

Only after grasping the impor-tance of this were we finally able to make steady progress in our relationship with Heather. When it was all said and done, we realized her behavior had nothing to do with the love we felt for her, or what she meant to us. Much like the leper, Heather was miserable. And because of her pain and unhappiness, she was making those around her unhappy as well. But just like the parent coping with a child with leprosy, my focus was not on the horrific disease but rather on its healing. In doing so, I was able to truthfully say, "I love you, Heather, simply because you are a person of immeasurable worth and you belong to me."

As a young teenager, Heather was often grounded because of a consequence. If she was grounded, however, she was never separated from the family. On more than one occasion, I used this as an opportunity for us to spend time together. Because Heather loved hats, we spent hours at the mall trying them on. True, I wasn't the friends with whom she wanted to hang out. However, I was better than no one, and this gave us a time to connect emotionally.

An interesting thing takes place once children truly begin to feel they belong. Because they feel loved, they begin to believe that they are worthy of being loved, and consequently begin to feel that they are worthwhile. Dr. Wagner says this sense of worthiness deals primarily with self-acceptance: "Worthiness is a feeling of 'I am good' or 'I count' or 'I am right.'"[5] It is the one thing that enables you to look in the mirror, like what you see, and feel significant.

Needing to feel important is another major variable for teen gang involvement, according to the University of Houston study.[6] Make sure you treat your child with importance and significance at home. Ask her for her thoughts or advice on a particular subject. Talk with her as you would a friend.

Finally Dr. Wagner stresses the importance of feeling capable or competent. "This is a feeling of adequacy, of courage, or hopefulness, of strength enough to carry out the task of daily life-situations. It is the 'I can' feeling of being able to face life and cope with its complexities."[7] The feeling of being capable is closely related to past successes in solving problems.

Initially we had helped Heather link her behavior with decisions she made. Up until this time, our focus had been only on bad behavior resulting from bad choices. We failed to see that she was making good decisions as well. We began to use the *Parenting Without Pressure* workbook to comment on daily stuff that was completed, contracts that were followed through, family rules that had been obeyed, and even bad behavior that was not repeated. Knowing that she was capable of making good choices and doing things right enabled her to gain self-confidence. And because this resulted in Heather feeling good about herself, it was something she wanted to repeat.

Additionally, we looked for other areas of competence and trained ourselves to look at the small steps, not just the finished picture. We realized that only by successfully mastering the smaller steps could she move on to bigger challenges. Many times we would say, "Honey, we are so proud of you. You have almost done it," or "You can do it. You've already done part of it," or even, "Sweetie, that was a great try, and you almost made it." We continually encouraged and motivated.

The feeling of competence is developed from having successes, both big and small. As a child masters the small steps, enlarge his steps accordingly. Always make sure those steps are enough to challenge but never enough to overwhelm him.

Working on making Heather feel she belonged, was worthwhile, and was competent, as well as giving her plenty of focused eye contact and appropriate physical contact provided a base on which she could grow as an individual and we could grow as a family.

ADDITIONAL WAYS TO SHOW UNCONDITIONAL LOVE

Appreciate the uniqueness of a child even if she has little in common with other family members. It is important for parents to validate children as individuals and not to assign importance to only those attributes that you find favorable. Unfortunately, some parents either verbally or nonverbally send messages that say, "Unless you are like me, you are not acceptable." You often see this with the fitness-freak parent who continually puts down an overweight child.

Parents should never allow their egos to get wrapped up in their children. It is astonishing how quickly parental focus can shift here. For example, when children are born,

> **WAYS TO SHOW UNCONDITIONAL LOVE**
>
> - Provide plenty of focused attention and appropriate physical contact.
> - Appreciate the uniqueness of each child.
> - Don't allow your ego to get wrapped up in the child.
> - Do whatever necessary to encourage a child's belief in himself.
> - Remember that a parent is like a mirror. The child sees herself as you see her.

parents quickly count fingers and toes and are delighted when everything is normal. But from that point on, some parents are never satisfied again. Instead, they long for the exceptional child who amazes and dazzles the world. Unfortunately, they quickly become addicted to the strokes they get from their child's successes.

Recently at a workshop, I encountered this with a family. Dad was furious because after years of great competitive skating, his son had decided to quit. The kid was tired of skating and wanted to try something else. Unfortunately, his dad was hooked on the trophy cabinet and the victory celebrations. Consequently, the child was made to feel like a failure simply because he no longer wanted to skate.

Finally, parents should do whatever is necessary to encourage a youngster's belief in himself. Never see a child as a problem, only a challenge. Help him be all he can be. Remember, as parents we are like mirrors to our children. As we see our children, they will see themselves. Psychologist William Glasser writes, "Children find in the eyes of their parents the mirror in which they define themselves in the relationship. Fill it with nothing, they become nothing. They have a tremendous ability to live down to the lowest expectation in any environment."[8]

Once I realized the importance of this, I consciously made sure that when Heather looked at me, I reflected the very best in her, as well as all the wonderful possibilities of what she could be.

IMPROVING ON THE FAMILY

I will never forget the sorrow in the voice of a mom as she told a group of parents that because of her divorce, she and her boys were no longer going to be a family. She was certain that the reality of family life would gradually disappear. Unfortunately, for her the word *family* meant having a mom and a dad and 3.2 kids living under the same roof, with a van in the garage and a dog in the doghouse.

If Dad Doesn't Live Here, Are We Still a Family?

Recent statistics tell us that this is no longer accurate. Half of all marriages end in divorce. And forty percent of all today's children will live with a single parent before they are eighteen. The term *family* is continually being redefined to include single moms, single dads, grandparents, aunts, uncles, and other kinds of extended family members living under the same roof. This single mom and her children are very definitely a family, but the quality of life her family experiences depends largely on her.

Remember, parents, that this is not a dress rehearsal. What you do with your family doesn't include the possibility of giving a better performance later. The life you live today for you and your children is all there is. Be it good or bad, tomorrow it is history. Make it good for yourself and for them.

Parental Commitment of Time

People spend time doing things they find most important. Or to put it a slightly different way, you make the time to do the things you really want to do.

Yet often, children rate very little of their parents' time. According to the University of Michigan's Institute of Social Research, working mothers spend a daily average of eleven minutes of quality time with their children during the weekdays and about thirty minutes on weekends. Fathers spend about eight minutes on weekdays and fourteen minutes on weekends. And for those moms who feel guilty about working, this startling statistic was discovered. Mothers who do not work outside the home average only thirteen minutes per day of quality time.[9]

Today many busy parents tend to buy instead of to spend; that is, they buy games, toys, and other things for their children instead of spending time with them. "I cannot be with you, but I will buy you something when I get home," are words often heard by children today.

Unstructured time. It takes time to get to know a young person, to feel her hurts and understand her problems. Parents continually need to look for opportunities to talk with their children, grabbing any chance they can find to share the lives of their kids. The key here is availability.

For Heather and me, the opportunity often came late at night. When Heather came in from a date, she was required to wake us up if we were asleep, as we usually were. Unfortunately for me, this was often the time she wanted to talk. Because I was determined not to miss my chance, we would sit at the kitchen table, laughing and talking well into the night. The mornings I left for work a little tired were a small price to pay for the late-night talks that have provided us both with some very warm memories.

Other opportunities of spending unstructured time with a child might include playing catch or shooting baskets, playing video games or board games, building a snowman or sand castle, helping with homework or daily chores, going for a walk, riding bikes, or simply reading a story.

Someone once said that love is spelled T-I-M-E. Time spent with children is an investment parents will never regret. Think of opportunities you might have to spend unstructured time with your children.

Structured time and making memories. In addition to grabbing every opportunity to spend unstructured time together, we also need to schedule time for the family. Spending time together provides the opportunity for happy memories from which the family can draw during difficult times.

In their excellent book *Crisis Proof Your Teenager*, Dr. Wibblesman and Kathleen McCoy state,

"Memories that last—and carry us through the trying times of adolescence and beyond—are usually of the simple everyday variety. Quite often they are treasure gifts of parental time and attention."[10] These might include summer picnics, backyard barbecues, or even learning a sport together as a family.

Yet few families spend time together. In fact, I was surprised to learn that many families do only two things together: they clean the house and mow the grass. Upon examining my own family, I realized that although we were a little better at family times than that, we did leave a great deal to chance.

Spontaneity is great. Few family times, however, result from last-minute planning. Family times need to be scheduled, something everyone in the family knows about and can prepare for. Preparation is especially handy with reluctant teenagers. Use arbitration as an opportunity to discuss and plan a monthly family time. Make it a priority and put it on the calendar.

Heather went through a stage when she didn't like going on family outings. Giving her time to mentally prepare helped greatly. And because Heather was a youngster capable of raining on a parade, we built in an incentive for her to have fun with the family. For every time she went with us and got along with other family members, she could bring a friend on the next outing. The interesting thing about Heather's reluctance to spend time with the family is that I don't ever remember her having a bad time.

Establishing Traditions

Often when we think of family rituals or traditions, we think only of moments from our childhood that closely resemble a Norman Rockwell painting. However, family traditions don't have to be old-fashioned or elaborate affairs. In fact, a family tradition can be very simple. The trick is discovering what is relevant to your family and works for you. Sometimes the warmest memories come from the simplest activities, such as preparing a special meal, Christmas Eve candlelight services, a day at the fair, celebrating promotions or school honors, working at the school carnival, or a special birthday celebration. Jennifer Allen writes in her article titled "The Incredible Healing Power of Family Rituals" that "the best rituals are really nothing more than a reflection of our desire to be close to one another."[11]

By having family fun times and establishing family traditions, parents make the time for sharing and recognize the importance of belonging to the family. Celebrating the family builds hopefulness and cements family ties.

Making Home a Safe Place

Home needs to be an emotionally safe place for all the family members. Everyone should be required to treat the others with respect. No exceptions! No one should ever be allowed to have a good time at the expense of another.

Like parents, children should not be allowed to emotionally abuse one another. Parents should immediately step in and stop combat between children lest somebody get physically hurt. Yet often they allow siblings to verbally obliterate one another. Verbal attacks may not cause physical injury, but they can bruise the spirit and can cause wounds that last a lifetime.

Parents are not going to be able to eliminate bickering among children. But they can discourage jealousy and unhealthy competition and should never tolerate a verbal onslaught. Teach your children that picking on one another is not an appropriate substitute for dealing with disagreements or eliminating boredom. More important, send a strong message that it will not be tolerated.

A mother who recently attended a PWOP workshop had an excellent idea for eliminating the verbal bashing that was going on between her children. She simply established a "no knock" rule. She charged fifty cents for every belittling or unkind statement that one child directed toward another. She followed through with the rule by having the child who was on the receiving end of the hurtful statement write in his workbook exactly what was said, who said it, and the time and date on which it was said. When allowances were paid on arbitration day, the mother deducted fifty cents for that statement from the allowance of the offending child.

What a great idea! The first week this rule was implemented, $12 changed hands. By the second week, however, the kids had caught on and only $2 changed hands. And soon her children were giving careful thought to what they said.

Teach your children constructive ways for dealing with disagreements with one another. Remind them that arbitration is an excellent means for

conflict resolution. In many households with teenage girls, for example, there is usually an ongoing conflict about clothes. My own teenage daughters were often caught in the conflict of what belonged to whom and who borrowed what. Instead of threats and harsh words, they hashed it out at arbitration and got everything back into the right closets.

Set this up to be a win-win proposition. Encourage your children to cooperate with one another, to get along and be team players. If a week goes by without any verbal bashing among family members, celebrate. Take the family to a movie or out for pizza. Again, set the family up to win. If verbal bashing has been ongoing behavior between the children in your family, start out by taking it a day at a time. And when they make it through the day without any verbal bashing, celebrate.

Remember, positively reinforced behavior is destined to be repeated. Most of the discord between youngsters is the result of sibling rivalry, much of which is to be expected. But as parents, you can help reduce it. Continually strive to hold each family member in high regard. Be careful not to single out one particular attribute of a child that you personally favor, such as playing a sport or making good grades. Instead, recognize each child for his or her special talents and qualities.

Assessing Your Family

Dr. Howard Hendricks, professor of Christian education at Dallas Theological Seminary, lists eight areas parents can examine to determine how healthy their families are. The closer parents come to accomplishing these eight things in their families, the healthier and happier they will be.[12]

"1. A healthy family is a caring family. It is a community of concerned people who assume unlimited liability for each other, who reach out to one another, and who build bridges instead of walls.

"2. A healthy family is a respectful family. Family members have a high regard for each other's uniqueness, and as a result, they are free to be open and honest. Many families claim they are open, but what they mean is that the children can say whatever they want to say provided the parents agree.

"3. A healthy family is convictional. The family is committed to a strong central value system and practices those values consistently. There is never a doubt on the part of a family member that they stand for honesty, loyalty, and integrity. Furthermore, it is not assumed that everyone knows what to do and why. Values are presented, explained, and discussed.

"4. A healthy family is a flexible family. It is free to change as the demands of society impinge on it. A family is flexible when the parents work together as a team. The parents are willing to admit mistakes, instead of taking irrational stands and spending the rest of their parenting days trying to defend them.

"5. A healthy family is an expressive family. This is different from caring—essentially what we do for others. Expression conveys the idea of how we respond to others, which includes feelings of warmth, affection, openness, and

understanding. There is less conflict and therefore more freedom to be oneself—freedom to make mistakes, to disagree, to laugh.

"6. A healthy family is a responsible family. Family members accept responsibility, and lines of communication are kept clear. In a responsible family, parents constantly are preparing their children for when they leave home. Then when the children do leave, the psychological umbilical cord has already been severed.

"7. A healthy family is an initiating family. The children and adults show a high level of initiative and energy by participating in a variety of constructive activities and interests. The family maintains community ties and is involved as a group and as individuals. Activities done as a family establish unity. Activities done separately establish individuality and distinctiveness.

"8. A healthy family is a realistic family. Realistic families see themselves as others see them. They are aware of what is going on in the world around them. They look at the world objectively."

Families are important. More than anything else, it is the family that socializes children; that is, teaches them society's rules and behavioral expectations. Additionally, from the family children learn morals, values, and attitudes. And they also learn about relationships and what is considered important. Parents teach these things to their children in three ways:

By experiencing. Day-by-day experiences teach children many lessons. For example, kids learn to

> ### CHECKLIST FOR A HEALTHY HOME
> Go through the list and assess your family. Where do you stand on these eight issues?
>
> **1.** Caring. Do you build bridges instead of walls?
> **2.** Respectful. Are people free to express their opinions?
> **3.** Convictional. Is your family committed to a central value system?
> **4.** Flexible. Are you willing to change the rules?
> **5.** Expressive. Do you respond warmly to those in your family?
> **6.** Responsible. Does each family member have some responsibility?
> **7.** Initiating. Is your family involved in outside activities, both individually and as a family?
> **8.** Realistic. Do you see your family as others do?

treat others respectfully by experiencing respect.

By teaching. Children also learn from verbal instruction. A parent, for example, may verbally instruct his child about the hazards of using drugs or alcohol.

By modeling. Finally, children learn simply by watching their parents. In fact, they learn far more by what their parents do than by what they say. For example, a parent may instruct a child about the merits of honesty. But the lasting impression will be created by the child's observation of the parent's honesty.

Almost everything parents do teaches children something about themselves and about life. Make very sure that your children are learning the life-lessons you intend to teach. Dorothy Law Nolte says it best:

A child that lives with criticism learns to condemn.

A child that lives with hostility learns to fight.

A child that lives with ridicule learns to be shy.

A child that lives with shame learns to be guilty.

A child that lives with affection learns to love.

A child that lives with tolerance learns to be patient.

A child that lives with encouragement learns confidence.

A child that lives with praise learns to appreciate.

A child that lives with fairness learns justice.

A child that lives with security learns faith.

A child that lives with approval learns to like himself/herself.

A child that lives with acceptance, learns to find love in the world.

HOMEWORK FOR PARENTS

1. Identify specific things you can do to show your children unconditional love. Commit yourself to doing at least one of these daily.

2. Plan at least one family-fun activity a month. This week at arbitration, discuss and plan the activity. Make it a family priority and follow through with it.

3. Identify values and attitudes that you believe are important and would like your children to learn. How are you teaching them to your children?

4. Identify and change those areas in your life that don't provide your children with a positive model for behavior.

PART TWO

THE FAMILY WORKBOOK

RULES WE CAN LIVE BY

1. Rule: _____
   _____
   _____

   Consequence: _____
   _____

2. Rule: _____
   _____
   _____

   Consequence: _____
   _____

3. Rule: _____
   _____
   _____

   Consequence: _____
   _____

4. Rule: _____
   _____
   _____

   Consequence: _____
   _____

5. Rule: _____
   _____
   _____

   Consequence: _____
   _____

6. Rule: _____
   _____
   _____

   Consequence: _____
   _____
   _____

RULES WE CAN LIVE BY

1. Rule: _____

_____

_____

Consequence: _____

_____

_____

2. Rule: _____

_____

_____

Consequence: _____

_____

_____

3. Rule: _____

_____

_____

Consequence: _____

_____

_____

4. Rule: _____

_____

_____

Consequence: _____

_____

_____

5. Rule: _____

_____

_____

Consequence: _____

_____

_____

6. Rule: _____

_____

_____

Consequence: _____

_____

_____

FRIENDS AND FAMILY

EMERGENCY NUMBERS
Police: 911   Fire: 911   Rescue Unit: 911

Family Doctor: _____

PARENTS AND RELATIVES
Mom at work: _____

Dad at work: _____

Relative: _____

Relative: _____

PARENTS' FRIENDS
Name and number: _____

Name and number: _____

Name and number: _____

Name and number: _____

NEIGHBORS
Name and number: _____

Name and number: _____

Name and number: _____

Name and number: _____

MY FRIENDS AND THEIR PARENTS
Friend's name and number: _____

Friend's parent and number: _____

Friend's name and number: _____

Friend's parent and number: _____

Friend's name and number: _____

Friend's parent and number: _____

FRIENDS AND FAMILY

EMERGENCY NUMBERS

Police: 911   Fire: 911   Rescue Unit: 911

Family Doctor: _____

PARENTS AND RELATIVES

Mom at work: _____

Dad at work: _____

Relative: _____

Relative: _____

PARENTS' FRIENDS

Name and number: _____

Name and number: _____

Name and number: _____

Name and number: _____

NEIGHBORS

Name and number: _____

Name and number: _____

Name and number: _____

Name and number: _____

MY FRIENDS AND THEIR PARENTS

Friend's name and number: _____

Friend's parent and number: _____

Friend's name and number: _____

Friend's parent and number: _____

Friend's name and number: _____

Friend's parent and number: _____

FUN TIMES AND EVENINGS OUT

Date: _____

Time leaving/returning: _____

Where I will be: _____

_____

Friends I will be with: _____

Date: _____

Time leaving/returning: _____

Where I will be: _____

_____

Friends I will be with: _____

Date: _____

Time leaving/returning: _____

Where I will be: _____

_____

Friends I will be with: _____

Date: _____

Time leaving/returning: _____

Where I will be: _____

_____

Friends I will be with: _____

Date: _____

Time leaving/returning: _____

Where I will be: _____

_____

Friends I will be with: _____

Date: _____

Time leaving/returning: _____

Where I will be: _____

_____

Friends I will be with: _____

FUN TIMES AND EVENINGS OUT

Date: _____

Time leaving/returning: _____

Where I will be: _____

_____

Friends I will be with: _____

Date: _____

Time leaving/returning: _____

Where I will be: _____

_____

Friends I will be with: _____

Date: _____

Time leaving/returning: _____

Where I will be: _____

_____

Friends I will be with: _____

Date: _____

Time leaving/returning: _____

Where I will be: _____

_____

Friends I will be with: _____

Date: _____

Time leaving/returning: _____

Where I will be: _____

_____

Friends I will be with: _____

Date: _____

Time leaving/returning: _____

Where I will be: _____

_____

Friends I will be with: _____

DAILY STUFF

Date: _____

Daily Stuff:

1. _____
2. _____
3. _____
4. _____
5. _____
6. _____
7. _____
8. _____
9. _____
10. _____

Messages:

_____
_____
_____
_____
_____
_____
_____
_____
_____
_____
_____
_____
_____
_____
_____
_____
_____
_____
_____

DAILY STUFF

Date: _____

Daily Stuff:

1. _____
2. _____
3. _____
4. _____
5. _____
6. _____
7. _____
8. _____
9. _____
10. _____

Messages:

_____
_____
_____
_____
_____
_____
_____
_____
_____
_____
_____
_____
_____
_____
_____
_____
_____
_____
_____

DAILY STUFF

Date: _____

Daily Stuff:

1. _____
2. _____
3. _____
4. _____
5. _____
6. _____
7. _____
8. _____
9. _____
10. _____

Messages:

_____
_____
_____
_____
_____
_____
_____
_____
_____
_____
_____
_____
_____
_____
_____
_____
_____
_____
_____

DAILY STUFF

Date: _____

Daily Stuff:

1. _____
2. _____
3. _____
4. _____
5. _____
6. _____
7. _____
8. _____
9. _____
10. _____

Messages:

_____
_____
_____
_____
_____
_____
_____
_____
_____
_____
_____
_____
_____
_____
_____
_____
_____
_____

DAILY STUFF

Date: _____

Daily Stuff:

1. _____
2. _____
3. _____
4. _____
5. _____
6. _____
7. _____
8. _____
9. _____
10. _____

Messages:

_____
_____
_____
_____
_____
_____
_____
_____
_____
_____
_____
_____
_____
_____
_____
_____
_____
_____

DAILY STUFF

Date: _____

Daily Stuff:

1. _____
2. _____
3. _____
4. _____
5. _____
6. _____
7. _____
8. _____
9. _____
10. _____

Messages:

_____
_____
_____
_____
_____
_____
_____
_____
_____
_____
_____
_____
_____
_____
_____
_____
_____
_____
_____

WEEKLY PROGRESS REPORT

Name: _____

For week of: _____

Class period	Subject	Teacher	Numerical grade point average
1st			
2nd			
3rd			
4th			
5th			
6th			

WEEKLY PROGRESS REPORT

Name: _____

For week of: _____

Class period	Subject	Teacher	Numerical grade point average
1st			
2nd			
3rd			
4th			
5th			
6th			

CONTRACT

Name: _____

Subject: _____

Desired Behavior: _____

_____

_____

How it will be accomplished: _____

_____

_____

Consequences: _____

_____

_____

_____

_____

_____

_____

_____

_____

_____

_____

_____

_____

_____

Child's Signature: _____   Date: _____

Parent's Signature: _____   Date: _____

CONTRACT

Name: _____

Subject: _____

Desired Behavior: _____

_____

_____

How it will be accomplished: _____

_____

_____

Consequences: _____

_____

_____

_____

_____

_____

_____

_____

_____

_____

_____

_____

_____

_____

_____

Child's Signature: _____ Date: _____

Parent's Signature: _____ Date: _____

THINGS TO DISCUSS
AT ARBITRATION

1. Date: _____
2. Date: _____
3. Date: _____
4. Date: _____
5. Date: _____
6. Date: _____
7. Date: _____
8. Date: _____

THINGS TO DISCUSS
AT ARBITRATION

1. Date: _____
2. Date: _____
3. Date: _____
4. Date: _____
5. Date: _____
6. Date: _____
7. Date: _____
8. Date: _____

THINGS TO DISCUSS
AT ARBITRATION

1. Date: _____
2. Date: _____
3. Date: _____
4. Date: _____
5. Date: _____
6. Date: _____
7. Date: _____
8. Date: _____

THINGS TO DISCUSS
AT ARBITRATION

1. Date: _____

2. Date: _____

3. Date: _____

4. Date: _____

5. Date: _____

6. Date: _____

7. Date: _____

8. Date: _____

THINGS TO DISCUSS
AT ARBITRATION

1. Date: _____

2. Date: _____

3. Date: _____

4. Date: _____

5. Date: _____

6. Date: _____

7. Date: _____

8. Date: _____

THINGS TO DISCUSS
AT ARBITRATION

1. Date: _____

2. Date: _____

3. Date: _____

4. Date: _____

5. Date: _____

6. Date: _____

7. Date: _____

8. Date: _____

ARBITRATION WORKSHEET

1. Define the problem. _____

_____

_____

_____

_____

2. Let the kids talk. _____

_____

_____

_____

_____

3. Let the parents talk. _____

_____

_____

_____

_____

4. Brainstorm possible solutions. _____

_____

_____

_____

_____

_____

5. Choose the best solution. _____

_____

_____

_____

_____

_____

6. How did it go? _____

_____

_____

_____

_____

_____

ARBITRATION WORKSHEET

1. Define the problem. _____
_____
_____
_____
_____

2. Let the kids talk. _____
_____
_____
_____
_____

3. Let the parents talk. _____
_____
_____
_____
_____

4. Brainstorm possible solutions. _____
_____
_____
_____
_____
_____

5. Choose the best solution. _____
_____
_____
_____
_____
_____

6. How did it go? _____
_____
_____
_____
_____
_____

Questions Parents Ask

For additional help getting started, I've included some of the most common questions about the workbook.

Q. Who writes in the children's workbooks and where do parents keep their notes?
A. Both parents and children write in the workbooks. Parents assign chores and write notes in "Daily Stuff." They also utilize "Anything and Everything Goes" to list arbitration topics. Kids use sections one through four to write their rules, list their friends, sign out before going out for the evening, and write notes to Mom and Dad. The important thing to remember, however, is that the workbook is simply a tool for the family. Utilize it in a way that works best for you!

Q. Can you use the program without making workbooks for your children?
A. Yes, but I recommend making the workbooks. It provides the structure and easy format to teach children the important concepts of accountability, responsibility, behavioral consequences, problem solving, and making good choices. Equally important, the workbook enables parents to easily shift their focus to what the children are doing right.

Q. Only one of our two children is giving us a tough time. Should we implement workbooks with both kids?
A. Yes. Not only does the workbook allow you to correct inappropriate behavior, it also serves as an excellent preventive tool for future problems.

Q. What age child is best suited for this program?
A. It works best with school-age children between the ages of six or seven and eighteen.

Q. Can you use the program with older kids who are in their late teens or early twenties? Our nineteen-year-old son needs it.
A. Absolutely. However, because of your son's age, I recommend that you use only the Rules We Can Live By and Daily Stuff sections. Also, weekly arbitrations are important.

After living on campus for three years, Heather moved back home during her senior year of college. Because she was an adult, we treated her as such. However, the workbook system again provided us with a safe structure. Everyone knew clearly what was expected of them. We had several basic household rules, and Heather was required to help with household chores that I assigned in the Daily Stuff section. Also, we consistently held weekly arbitrations to deal with small situations before they became big problems.

Q. When I suggested starting the program and workbook, my teenager just laughed. Now what?
A. Don't suggest. Inform your teen that you're going to implement the program and the workbook, which will eliminate fighting. Also inform him that this program is fair because it deals with tangible measures and will give him more control over what he can and cannot do.

Q. We have been implementing the workbook system for several months. However, many times my teenage son still doesn't remember to complete his daily stuff, which means I end up doing it. Any suggestions?
A. Determine why he's not completing his daily stuff. Are you being sensitive to his school schedule? Does he have adequate time? If his explanation is that he forgets, inform him that his memory lapse is no excuse and try the following: (1) Formulate a rule/consequence concerning daily stuff that includes a specific time for each task to be completed. (2) Give other children in the family the opportunity to complete his assigned task for money (one dollar per item, which

is then deducted from his allowance). If this generates discord among the kids, simply complete the task and pay yourself. (3) Remind your son that this is an area of responsibility that will be examined at arbitration when he wants extended privileges.

Q. How do you handle a crisis situation that occurs during the week and your arbitration is on the weekend?
A. If possible, apply your disobeying rule. Heather's disobeying rule stated: "Any willful act of disobedience will result in being grounded until the next arbitration." At that meeting, we discussed the problem and, if needed, the additional consequence. This eliminated immediately addressing a serious problem when we felt angry and hadn't thought it through. However, if the crisis warrants immediate attention, take enough time to get your emotions in check and then call an emergency arbitration.

Q. What do you do if a child destroys his workbook or it disappears?
A. Always make the child responsible for his workbook. If it disappears, he is responsible for its replacement cost and for duplicating the information it contained. If he destroyed the workbook, then in addition to the above, either his disobeying rule with its consequence would apply or he could lose all TV and phone privileges for a week.

Q. Recently I asked my daughter to do a few extra things that I had not included in her Daily Stuff section. She said she didn't have to do them because they were not on her list. Is she right?

A. The fairness of the program wins over kids more quickly than anything else. Consequently, be as fair as possible. Imagine having your boss continually add to your list of assigned tasks. Just when you thought you were making progress, he adds several more items. That is how kids feel when you add to their lists. However, having said all that, you are the parent and you have the right to make additional requests. But the requests should be important and I wouldn't do this often.

Q. Should we have workbooks for my husband's children when they stay with us on alternating weekends?

A. No. You do have a right, however, to expect them to follow your household rules. Always make sure you have defined these rules before you enforce them.

Q. For years my son has fed his dog. Since we started the workbook system, he doesn't do it unless it is listed. Now what?

A. List feeding the dog as part of his daily stuff chores. Or give him the choice of feeding the dog with or without a rule and a consequence.

Parenting Problems and Solutions
Confronting the frequently asked questions

As I've taught Parenting Without Pressure workshops through the years, participants frequently tell me about their children's behavioral problems and ask for solutions. I've listened, helped brainstorm workable solutions—and learned that kids find creative ways to frustrate their parents!

On the following pages, I've described some problems and my suggestions for their resolution. Maybe you'll find yourself in a few of these situations and hopefully the solutions will work for you. But remember: success depends on parents being firm and consistent with discipline while providing plenty of unconditional love.

Problem: Alex's Temper Tantrum
Alex has no regard for the personal property of others. Often when he's angry, he gets destructive. He punches holes in walls and breaks things. One time he became so furious with his sister that he broke my cellular phone by throwing it across the family room. Alex says he can't control his temper. I say he won't. What do you say?

Solution: I say Alex has a right to his feelings. However, he does not have the right to always act on them.

At arbitration, carefully explain to Alex that throwing and smashing things are not acceptable ways to deal with frustration and anger. Make it clear that you will no longer tolerate his destructive behavior. Establish a rule that says, "If you damage or destroy other people's property, you will make restitution. If you throw a tantrum and damage other people's property, you will make restitution and be grounded for a week. If Alex's destructive outbursts continue, seek professional help.

Problem: Sally's Disaster Area
To say Sally's bedroom is a wreck is an understatement. It looks more like a toxic-waste site. We fight about it constantly because I can't stand the mess. On several occasions, I got so frustrated that I cleaned it myself. My husband tells me to close the bedroom door and forget it. That's hard for me to do. I want the room cleaned up. What do you suggest?

Solution: I had a similar problem with Heather for years. But finally I hit on a solution. We wrote a rule that said, "Every morning before school, your bed must be made and all towels picked up and hung in the bathroom." As a consequence for not doing this, I charged Heather $1.00 for an unmade bed and 75 cents per wet towel. During the week, I let everything else go. And as your husband suggested to you, I shut her bedroom door.

However, every Saturday I required Heather to clean her room. Because her idea of "clean" was different from mine, I developed a list of tasks to complete. For example: clean under and behind the bed; change the bed sheets; pick up everything on the floor and put it in the proper place; dust and straighten the top of the desk and dresser; vacuum the carpet; vacuum and organize the closet floor. Then after Heather cleaned, I checked the list to decide if the room looked satisfactory.

Problem: Shage's Shoplifting
Recently the police arrested our fourteen-year-old daughter for shoplifting. Shage is a nice girl and has never been in trouble before. Needless to say, we are heartsick. What is the best way to deal with this?

Solution: As tough as it is, allow Shage to suffer the results of her actions. She must learn that her behavior has consequences and that most businesses prosecute to the fullest extent of the law for shoplifting.

Then determine the reason for Shage's behavior and specifically address the problem. Was she trying to gain peer acceptance? Kids who struggle with poor self-esteem are more vulnerable to negative peer pressure. Did she shoplift to get a "high" from doing it? Kids sometimes shoplift for excitement and the satisfaction of not getting caught. Was

she stealing things her budget would not allow her to buy? Kids with limited resources sometimes steal items such as CDs or clothing. Or was she seeking attention and asking for help? Shoplifting is a red flag that says, "Something is wrong here. I need help." Shage may need professional counseling.

In addition to the legal consequences, I would apply your disobeying rule. Also, I would tell Shage to write a 250 to 500-word essay about the many problems associated with teenage shoplifting. Discuss the essay with her and what she's learned from this episode.

Problem: Lance's Constant Lies
My teenage son Lance lies so much, I never know when he's telling the truth. What should I do?

Solution: Explain to Lance that lying can become a habit, that it never pays, and it destroys your trust. Then establish a rule and consequence about the lying.

More important, uncover why your child lies to you. For instance, some kids from rigid, authoritarian homes feel they must lie to get breathing room. Or if Mom and Dad are quick to say no to friends and activities, kids may quit asking and start lying.

It's wiser for parents to say yes as much as possible and then work with their children on good decision making and trust building. When determining whether to say yes or no, ask the questions from chapter 3: Is this illegal? Is it immoral? Is it inappropriate for his age? Is it going to hurt him or someone else? Is it going to make a difference in five years? If the answer to these questions is no, then it's probably OK to say yes.

Children also lie because of poor self-esteem. They create fantasies that plug the holes in their fragile egos. For example, kids can tell elaborate tales to their friends just to impress them. Maybe Lance needs you to help build his self-esteem.

Other children lie to postpone punishment, especially when consequences aren't fair and reasonable. Are your rules and consequences appropriate for his age, personality, and circumstances?

And unfortunately, kids sometimes lie because they've been taught to by their parents. Check your own behavior. Have you modeled the message that lying is acceptable? For example, have you ever asked a family member to lie on your behalf? Or have your kids heard you lie to others? It's important to remember that kids learn more by watching your behavior than by listening to your verbal instructions.

Problem: Julie's Questionable Friends

Our daughter Julie is hanging out with some questionable kids. Her grades have dropped and lately she's been surly and disrespectful. My husband wants to snoop through her things. I think it would be an invasion of her privacy. What do you think?

Solution: For teenagers, privacy is a privilege, not a right. If she's behaving well, respect her privacy. However, if things are shaky, it's time to look around. If you want to know how your daughter is doing, first consider her best friend. Chances are, Julie is doing the same things

as her friend.

If you suspect drug or alcohol abuse or other dangerous behavior, you need to look further. Going through a child's drawers, closet, and personal items is difficult, so please don't do it when everything is fine. But sometimes, for the sake of your child's life, it's a must.

Problem: Danny's Phantom Illness

Danny often complains of feeling sick on school days or when I've given him chores around the house. Ironically, he makes a remarkable recovery when he wants to do something with his friends in the evening. I feel he's manipulating me. What can I do about this?

Solution: Buy a thermometer and establish a rule that says, "Unless you have a temperature of 100 degrees or more, you will go to school or complete your assigned task. The only exception is if you're vomiting. If you do stay home from school or if you don't complete your assigned task because of illness, you'll need to rest. You won't be allowed to see your friends or go out with them on the days you stay home." Tough as it sounds, this rule usually eliminates phantom illnesses.

Problem: Laurie's Door Slamming

Every time Laurie gets angry with someone in the family, she runs to her room, slams the door, and locks it. I don't mind Laurie going to her room, but when she slams the door, the entire house shakes. Any suggestions?

Solution: At arbitration, carefully

explain to Laurie that slamming doors is no longer acceptable. Then simply establish a rule that says, "You may not slam doors." The consequence? Remove the door for a week.

Problem: Brian's Money Grabbing

Last week, my sixteen-year-old son took $20 from my purse. I took Brian's boom box until he repaid me, but with no results. Then I took his $150 athletic shoes . . . still no results. I don't think he cares. What now?

Solution: A parent who attended a PWOP workshop had a similar problem. Her solution worked well and can help you. During arbitration, inform Brian that he's never to take money from your purse. To do so is stealing. As a consequence for taking your $20, give him seven days to complete two things. (1) Repay you the $20. If he doesn't have a job, provide chores for him and pay minimum wage. If he does not repay you at the end of the week, take his boom box to the pawn shop and hock it for the $20. It will be his responsibility to retrieve it. (2) Assign to Brian a 500-word essay on what it means to steal; what it feels like to have something stolen; what consequences are reaped for stealing in the "real world."

Problem: Aaron's Bad Mouth

My son has a mouth you wouldn't believe! His swearing upsets me. Any suggestions?

Solution: Establish a rule that says "No swearing allowed." Then make sure he understands what you consider to be swearing. The consequence would depend on your son's age. A younger child can write 50 to 100 times, "I will not use profanity," or write a 200-word essay on why he shouldn't swear. The assignment must be completed before he can eat dinner, which will be served at the dinner hour only. If the assignment isn't completed, he misses dinner.

For a teenager, charge $5 per offending word. If his allowance does not cover the account balance, give him a list of chores and pay minimum wage for doing them.

Problem: Stacy's Slipping Out

I've just learned that Stacy, my sixteen-year-old daughter, is slipping out at night. Apparently she waits until everyone is asleep and then sneaks out her bedroom window. I don't want to permanently lock her bedroom windows in case of a fire, but what else can a parent do?

Solution: Let Stacy know that slipping out at night is a major breach of trust. As a consequence, for the next three weeks she'll be on restriction. Also inform her that from now on during the night you'll set your alarm and periodically check that she's in her room. If the problem continues, install an alarm system so every time a window or door opens at night, the alarm goes off.

Problem: Michelle's Phone Use

In your workshops, you mention that parents can revoke phone privileges as a consequence. We'd like to use this method with our daughter Michelle, but my husband and I don't get home until 6:30 in the evening. How can we enforce a phone restriction if we're not at the house in the afternoon? Also, we have other children and don't want to remove the phone completely.

Solution: There are a couple of things that you can do. First, if Michelle has lost this privilege, you can ask her not to use the phone. Ideally, she will comply. However, if she disobeys, many phone companies offer a service called "phone block." It enables you to block unauthorized phone calls, particularly those from your child's friends. You can also buy a machine called the "Command Communication Phone Sitter" from a local store. It blocks unauthorized phone calls and it's easy to install.

Problem: Mandy's Refusal to Arbitrate

You suggest holding a weekly arbitration with children. However, every time I mention arbitration to my teenage daughter, Mandy, she tells me to forget it.

Solution: This problem sounds similar to a mother's situation who recently attended a workshop. She felt at a loss about how to involve her daughter in arbitration. The following solution worked well for her.

This mother told her daughter that she'd shop for groceries only after they successfully held a Saturday morning arbitration to establish household rules. Her daughter told her to forget it. Consequently, the mom didn't shop for groceries. Actually, this worked well for the mother because she wanted to lose some weight. Every morning on her way to work, she purchased two diet drink meal supplements and on the way home, she purchased a diet meal and a salad from the deli.

After a few days when the bread, milk, and cereal disappeared, the daughter asked, "When are you going grocery shopping?" The mom replied, "I don't know? When are we going to have an arbitration?"

The daughter held out longer and when the soup, Spam, and sardines in the back of the pantry were gone, she asked again, "When are you going to get groceries?" Her mother answered, "It's up to you. When are we going to have an arbitration?" Mandy held out for ten days and finally felt ready to talk.

One word of caution. Parental attitude is very important. Make sure you're communicating this: "I love you and arbitration can work for both of us."

Problem: Jason's Morning Tardiness

My eight-year-old Jason constantly makes me late for work. I can't get him out of bed on time. And because he takes his sweet time and dawdles, I end up frustrated and screaming at him. I'm at a loss for what to do.

Solution: Inform your son that you're no longer going to be late for work. From now on, you'll leave the house at exactly 8:00 in the morning and whatever shape he's in at that time is the way he'll go to school. Make a list of things he must accomplish before breakfast, such as washing his face, brushing his teeth, getting dressed, combing his hair, and making his bed. Allow him to put a big check by each accomplished task and if he accomplishes all of them, give him a token. When he acquires five tokens, take Jason to his favorite fast-food restaurant on Friday after school.

Recently, a mom who attended a

Parenting Without Pressure workshop had a similar problem. But the son realized she meant business after he arrived at school with a shoe on one foot and only a sock on the other. Her son explained the sock by telling friends that he hurt his foot. After that experience, though, he got ready on time in the morning.

Problem: Toni's School Detentions

I car pool with several other middle-school mothers. Toni, my thirteen-year-old daughter, constantly earns detentions for being late to class because she spends too much time talking with friends. Consequently, between the car pool and picking up Toni from detention, I spend the afternoon in my car. I'm tired of it! I've tried taking away her phone and it doesn't work. What do you suggest?

Solution: I'd give the problem back to Toni. You've already arranged daily transportation to and from school via the car pool. If because of her behavior Toni gets a detention, make her responsible for transportation home. Three options come to mind. (1) Toni can walk home, but you might not feel comfortable if the neighborhood isn't safe. (2) She can call a cab and pay the fare from her allowance or by working for you at minimum wage. (3) Determine the cab fare and charge her that amount when your family member picks up Toni from school.

Problem: Dean and Darcy's Stuff

When my two teenagers, Dean and Darcy, return home from school, they start shedding their stuff at the door. Jackets, book bags, shoes, purses, hair brushes. You name it, it's tossed in this corner and that. When I get home from work, the house is a wreck and I get angry. Is it too much to ask kids to pick up after themselves?

Solution: No, it's not too much to ask. But for most teens, picking up their things is a learned behavior. You need to establish a rule that says, "You must pick up your things and put them in your room. The consequence: If Mom picks up your things, they are hers for a week."

As you pick up your kids' belongings, place each item in a paper bag and staple the top shut. With a marker, write on each bag the owner's name and when that item will be returned. However, remember that a good consequence is one that works. If taking the item for a week doesn't work, try charging one or two dollars for each belonging. The amount can be deducted from an allowance, lunch money, or the money from a part-time job.

Problem: Benjamin's Scattered Toys

I have a similar problem, except it's not books and hair brushes, but toys. The battle begins when I ask seven-year-old Benjamin to pick up his toys and put them away.

Solution: It sounds as though you're locked in a power struggle. Give up the struggle. Buy a kitchen timer. Then carefully explain to Benjamin that he has fifteen minutes to pick up his toys. Anything not picked up when the timer goes off gets put in a "Sunday box." Toys in this box can be reclaimed only on Sunday. In the meantime, work overtime on rewarding behavior that you want repeated. Every time he picks up his toys, thank him.

Problem: Jon's School Fights

My son Jon is a high school student who's frequently in fist fights at school and already he's been suspended twice this year. Mr. Tough Guy then sits at home watching television and eating me out of house and home. I'm afraid he's going to fail the ninth grade again. What can I do?

Solution: First, find out what's going on at school and determine why your son fights. Kids who chronically act out usually have a problem in at least one of several areas. For example, is he academically capable of doing the work? A teen who struggles with studies may go to any length to avoid admitting the problem. Socially, is he teased by other kids? Or have they learned that Jon has a short fuse and they bait him until he throws a punch? Is Jon wrestling with something related to home life and acting it out at school?

Talk with Jon about what causes him to fight. Then explain that fighting is not an appropriate way to deal with frustration. Discuss other ways to resolve conflict and deal with anger such as walking away, counting to ten, talking with a teacher or guidance counselor, or calling you on the phone.

Establish a rule and consequence about physical fighting that says, "You may not physically fight. If you do fight—and especially if you're suspended for fighting—you will spend your days at home working." Chores might include yard work, painting, digging up a garden, cleaning the basement, cleaning the garage, or other manual labor.

I would make it worthwhile for him to resolve his problems and not get suspended from school. Add an incentive: "For every week that you don't get in trouble at school and earn a 2.0 grade point average, I will. . . ." Help him identify what it feels like to behave correctly. If the fighting continues, seek professional counseling.

Problem: Tracy Runs Away from Home

Tracy, who is fifteen years old, ran away from home two days ago and we're frantic. Things have been rough at home, but we didn't expect her to leave. What should we do?

Solution: Running away is serious and a big "red flag" for parents. Several steps should be taken immediately.

1. Contact your child's friends and their parents. Most runaways travel fewer than ten miles from home and stay with friends. Ask them to notify you immediately if they hear from Tracy. Let them know that she doesn't have permission to be anywhere but home.

2. Notify the police. Provide them with a recent photo and description.

3. Call the runaway organizations. Call the National Center for Missing and Exploited Children: 1-800-843-5678. This organization will provide you with immediate assistance in locating your child. Also contact the National Runaway Switchboard for counseling and referral services: 1-800-621-4000. And try the National Runaway Hotline for possible messages from your daughter: 1-800-231-6946. Have someone stay by the phone with a pencil and paper in case Tracy calls you.

Once Tracy returns home and everyone calms down, you'll need to resolve the things that you describe as "rough at home." Identify the problem(s). Children run away *from* something rather than *to* something. She may have run because of a breakdown in communication and constant fighting between her and you. She could feel like no one cares and that life at home is a big hassle to avoid. Or a family crisis could have motivated her to leave, such as alcohol, drug use, separation, divorce, death, or another disruption. Or possibly it's the fear of physical, emotional, or sexual abuse.

On the other hand, running away can be an escape for a teen overwhelmed by her own problems. These may include alcohol, drug use, failing in school, or a variety of other reasons. Talk to Tracy about what caused her to run, letting her vent feelings that you may not agree with.

Express your love and concern and your willingness to deal with whatever caused her to leave. Let her know that every problem has a solution and that you are committed as a family to finding the right one.

Problem: Rick's Bag of Pot
Yesterday when I put my son Rick's clothes away, I found a plastic bag of pot. He says it's nothing to worry about because he only smokes it occasionally—and at least he's not dropping acid like his friends. I'm horrified and worried sick. I don't want to overreact, but what should I do?

Solution: Let your son know that drug use of any kind won't be permitted under any circumstances. Then explore the depth of the problem.

There are four levels of drug use. They are (1) experimentation: using drugs once or twice, just to discover what they're like; (2) recreational or social: using drugs while with friends; (3) substance abuse: using drugs to escape from reality; (4) addiction: using drugs because they control the person's life and become the top priority. To determine the level of Rick's drug use, you may need the help of a professional.

If your son is experimenting or using drugs socially, you might modify his behavior by establishing a rule and consequence, plus taking him to counseling. Random drug screenings also may be necessary to monitor his drug use. However, if he's using drugs as an escape or seems drug dependent, intensive therapy or hospitalization might be needed.

Problem: Ethan's Bullying Classmate
A classmate at school bullies my thirteen-year-old, Ethan. So far, it's just been verbal teasing and nothing physical. I've told my son to ignore the kid because Ethan's reaction is half of the bully's good time. Ethan has trouble doing this. What do you suggest?

Solution: It's important to validate your son's feelings. His pain over being bullied is real and he needs to know that you understand. After this, talk about his reaction and its payoff to the bully. Discuss how to eliminate the payoff by ignoring the bully's teasing. Then make this new behavior worth your son's efforts.

Every time he walks away from

the bully without comment, reward Ethan with plenty of praise and tangible incentives. Great incentives for a young teen include tokens for video games, money for skateboard hardware, passes to movies, or even an extra allotment of Mom's or Dad's time on a Saturday. If the bullying continues, intervene and get help from the school.

Notes

Introduction
1. Geraldine Youcha and Judith Seixas, "Drinking, Drugs, and Children," *Parents*, March 1989, page 146.

2. Ann Landers, "Time to Wake Up to Kids' Troubles," *The Orlando Sentinel*, November 18, 1990, page F-12.

3. Jon D. Hull, "A Boy and His Gun," *Time*, August 2, 1993, page 22.

4. Landers, F-12.

5. Landers, F-12.

6. Greg Cynaumon, *Helping Single Parents with Troubled Kids* (Colorado Springs, CO: NavPress, 1992), page 138.

7. Diane Salvatore, "The Truth About Teens and Drinking," *Ladies Home Journal*, January 1988, page 105.

Chapter One
1. Beth Winship, "Traits Teen Should Learn on Their Way to Maturity," *The Orlando Sentinel*, January 1, 1987, page E-6. Used with permission.

Chapter Two
1. William R. Brown, "Relationships Between Abuse of Alcohol/Drugs and Juvenile Offenders," *Report for Metropolitan Alcoholism Council of Central Florida*, Orlando, FL, March 1987, page 40.3.

2. Guy LaFrancois, *The Lifespan* (Belmount, CA: Wadsworth Publishing Company 1993), page 285.

3. Caryl Waller Krueger, *Working Parent Happy Child* (Nashville, TN: Abingdon Press, 1990), page 20.

4. Robert Wallace, "Responsibility Paves Way to Freedom," *The Orlando Sentinel*, September 18, 1990, Style Section.

5. LaFrancois, page 417.

Chapter Three
1. James Dobson, *The Strong Willed Child* (Wheaton, IL: Tyndale, 1987), pages 29-33.

Chapter Four
1. Rudolf Dreikurs, *Children: The Challenge* (New York, NY: Penguin Books, 1964), pages 76-81.

Chapter Five

1. Lee and Marlene Carter, *Assertive Discipline for Parents* (New York, NY: Harper and Row Publishers, 1985), page 19.

2. Thomas Gordon, as quoted by Don Dinkmeyer and Gary D. Mckay in *The Parent's Guide* for STEP (Systematic Training for Effective Parenting of Teens) (Circle Pines, MN: American Guidance Service, 1983), page 103.

Chapter Six

1. David Veerman, "Roller Coaster Kids," *Parents and Teenagers*, ed. Jay Kesler with Ronald Beers (Wheaton, IL: Victor Books, 1984), page 198.

2. James E. Gardner, *Understanding, Helping, Surviving the Turbulent Teens* (San Diego, CA: Oak Tree Publications, Inc., 1982), page 181.

3. Kevin Leman, *Smart Kids, Stupid Choices* (Ventura, CA: Regal Books, 1987), page 110.

4. Kathleen McCoy and Charles Wibbelsman, M.D., *Crisis Proof Your Teenager* (New York, NY: Bantam Books, 1991), page 124.

5. Dan Korem, *Streetwise Parents, Foolproof Kids* (Colorado Springs, CO: NavPress, 1992), page 171.

6. James Dobson, *Preparing for Adolescence* (Santa Ana, CA: Vision House, 1978), page 21.

7. Ross Campbell, *How to Really Love Your Teenager* (Wheaton, IL: Victor Books, 1985), page 25.

8. David Veerman, "Skin Deep—Preoccupation with Physical Appearance," *Parents and Teenagers*, ed. Jay Kesler with Ronald Beers (Wheaton, IL: Victor Books, 1984), page 180. Used by permission.

9. Veerman, page 180.

10. Veerman, page 180.

11. Veerman, page 181.

12. Veerman, page 181.

13. Fritz Ridenour, *What Teenagers Wish Their Parents Knew About Kids* (Waco, TX: Word Book Publisher, 1982), page 48.

14. Barbara Gregg, "100 Ways for Parents to Show Appreciation," *Seminole Outlook*, January 5, 1989. Used by permission.

15. Ridenour, page 48.

16. Ridenour, page 49.

Chapter Seven

1. National Commission on Excellence in Education, "A Nation at Risk: The Imperative for Education Reform" (Washington, DC: Department of Education, 1983), page 35.

2. Susan Barbieri, "Dropout: A Matter of Self-Esteem," *The Orlando Sentinel*, March 30, 1990, page E-14.

Chapter Eight

1. Merrill Raber and George Dyck, *Mental Fitness: A Guide to Emotional Health* (Los Altos, CA: Crisp Publications, 1987), pages 45-46. Used by permission.

2. P. Jakubowski and A. J. Lane, *The Assertive Option* (Champaign, IL: Research Press), pages 80-81.

3. Pam Smith, *Eat Well, Live Well* (Lake Mary, FL: Creation House, 1992), page 55.

4. Mary Durkin, *Making Your Family Work* (Chicago, IL: The Thomas More Association, 1988), page 55.

5. Christian Hageseth, as quoted by Ellen Javernick in "He Who Laughs Last," *Parents Magazine*, September 1989, page 6.

Chapter Nine

1. Ross Campbell, *How to Really Love Your Teenager* (Wheaton, IL: Victor Books, 1985), page 45.

2. Campbell, page 48.

3. Maurice Wagner, *The Sensation of Being Somebody* (Grand Rapids, MI: Zondervan Publishing House, 1975), page 34.

4. Greg Wallace, "Gang Member Speaks Out on Esteem," *The Orlando Sentinel*, Talking with Teens—Style Section.

5. Wagner, page 34.

6. Wallace.

7. Wagner, page 36.

8. William Glasser, as quoted by Stephanie Marston in *The Magic of Encouragement* (New York, NY: Pocket Books, 1990), page 215.

9. Marston, page 69.

10. Kathleen McCoy and Charles Wibbelsman, *Crisis Proof Your Teenager* (New York, NY: Bantam Books, 1991), page 62.

11. Jennifer Allen, "The Incredible Healing Power of Family Rituals," *McCalls*, February 1993, page 73.

12. Howard Hendricks, "It's Time for a Checkup," *Parents and Teenagers*, ed. Jay Kesler with Ronald Beers (Wheaton, IL: Victor Books, 1984), pages 24-25. Used by permission.

Bibliography

CAMPBELL, ROSS
How to Really Love Your Teenager. Wheaton, IL: Victor Books, 1985.

CARTER, LEE AND MARLENE
Assertive Discipline for Parents. New York: Harper & Row, 1985.

CLINE, FOSTER, M.D., AND FAY, JIM
Parenting with Love and Logic. Colorado Springs, CO: Piñon Press, 1992.

COLEN, ROBERT, AND STOKES, GEOFFREY
Sex and the American Teenager. New York: Harper and Row, 1985.

DINKMEYER, DON, AND MCKAY, GARY D.
The Parent's Guide for STEP (Systematic Training for Effective Parenting of Teens). Circle Pines, MN: American Guidance Service, 1983.

DOBSON, JAMES
Preparing for Adolescence, third edition. Santa Ana, CA: Vision House, 1980.

DOBSON, JAMES
The Strong Willed Child. Wheaton, IL: Tyndale House, 1981.

DREIKUS, RUDOLF, M.D.
Children: The Challenge. A Plume Book, 1990.

DURKIN, MARY G.
Making Your Family Work. Chicago, IL: Thomas More Press, 1988.

FABER, ADELE, AND MAZLISH, ELAINE
How to Talk So Kids Will Listen and Listen So Kids Will Talk. New York: Avon Books, 1982.

FABER, ADELE, AND MAZLISH, ELAINE
Liberated Parents—Liberated Children. New York: Avon Books, 1975.

GARDNER, JAMES E.
Understanding, Helping, Surviving the Turbulent Teens. San Diego, CA: Oak Tree Publications, 1982.

GLENN, STEPHEN H., AND NELSEN, JANE, ED.D.
Raising Self-Reliant Children in a Self-Indulgent World. Rocklin, CA: Prima Publishing & Communication, 1989.

JAKUBOWSKI, P., AND LANE, A.J.
The Assertive Option. Champaign, IL: Research Press.

KESLER, JAY, WITH BEERS, RONALD
Parents and Teenagers. Wheaton, IL: Victor Books, 1984.

KOLODNY, ROBERT C. AND NANCY; BRATTER, THOMAS; AND DEEP, CHERYL
How to Survive Your Adolescent's Adolescence. Boston, MA: Little, Brown & Co., 1984.

KRUGER, CARYL WALLER
Working Parent, Happy Child. Nashville, TN: Abingdon Press, 1990.

LEMAN, KEVIN
Smart Kids, Stupid Choices. Ventura, CA: Regal Books, 1987.

MAGID, KEN, M.D., AND MCKELVERY, CAROLE A.
High Risk: Children Without a Conscience. New York: Bantam Books, 1988.

MCCOY, KATHY
The Teenage Survival Guide. New York: Simon and Schuster, 1981.

MCDOWELL, JOSH
Why Wait? What You Need to Know About Teen Sexuality. San Bernardino, CA: Here's Life Publishers, 1987.

NELSON, JANE, ED.D.
Positive Discipline. New York: Ballantine Books, 1981.

RABER, MERRILL, AND DYCK, GEORGE
Mental Fitness—A Guide to Emotional Health. Los Altos, CA: Crisp Publications.

RIDENOUR, FRITZ
What Teenagers Wish Their Parents Knew About Kids. Waco, TX: Word, 1982.

WEINHAUS, EVONNE, AND FRIEDMAN, KAREN
Stop Struggling with Your Teen. New York: Penguin Books, 1988.

WESSON, CAROLYN MCLENAHAN
Teen Troubles: How to Keep Them from Becoming Tragedies. New York: Walker and Co., 1988.

WINSHOP, BETH
"Traits Teens Should Learn on Their Way to Maturity," *The Orlando Sentinel*, January 1, 1987.

YOUNGS, BETTIE B.
A Stress-Management Guide for Young People. Del Mar, CA: Bilicki Publications, 1986.

Author

When her first husband died in the Vietnam War, Teresa Langston was catapulted into circumstances that were quite different from the ideal life she had planned. Suddenly she was a grieving and devastated widow and a single mother of an eighteen-month-old daughter. She subsequently married a man with three children, and soon had another daughter. As she experienced firsthand the challenges of parenthood, she began a journey that led to the Parenting Without Pressure philosophy.

A graduate of the University of Central Florida, Teresa Langston is recognized nationally for her expertise in the parenting field. A writer, speaker, and workshop leader since 1987, she resides in Longwood, Florida, with her husband, Herbert.